WHAT IS
SHORT SELLING?

TOM TAULLI

McGraw-Hill

New York Chicago San Francisco Lisbon
London Madrid Mexico City Milan New Delhi
San Juan Seoul Singapore Sydney Toronto

1234567890 AGM/AGM 0987654

ISBN 0-07-142785-6

Library of Congress Cataloging-in-Publication Data.

Taulli, Tom, 1968-
    What is short selling? / by Tom Taulli.
        p.   cm.
    ISBN 0-07-142785-6 (pbk. : alk. paper)
    1. Short selling.   2. Speculation.   I. Title.
HG6041.T382   2004
332.64'5—dc22
                                              2003016485

CONTENTS

INTRODUCTION

To enjoy the advantages of a free market, one must have both buyers and sellers, both bulls and bears. A market without bears would be like a nation without a free press. There would be no one to criticize and restrain the false optimism that always leads to disaster.

—BERNARD BARUCH, FAMED INVESTOR, IN A 1917 STATEMENT BEFORE THE COMMITTEE ON RULES OF THE HOUSE OF REPRESENTATIVES

Short selling has an underworld quality about it. One reason is that many investors do not understand the concept or processes involved in shorting stock. There is an intricate process used to short stocks, such as setting up a margin account, borrowing stock, dealing with the so-called "uptick rule," and so on.

Besides, short selling sounds counterintuitive. How is it possible to make money when a stock price falls in value?

Then there is the moral question. If a short seller is making money when many others are losing their shirts, is this fair? Is this wrong? Many investors think so—as well as legislators (some countries have altogether eliminated the practice of short selling on moral grounds).

No question, short selling is controversial—and always has been. This will not change. For example, during World War I, there was fear that German Kaiser Wilhelm II would surreptitiously short the U.S. markets and cause turmoil.

In fact, after September 11th, there was an investigation as to whether Osama bin Laden was shorting insurance and airline stocks before the planes hit the Twin Towers in New York City. (Investigations uncovered no evidence of this.)

This book is not about to prove whether short selling is right or wrong. Rather, this book explains the concept and mechanics of short selling, as well as the strategies. We also look at the risk factors.

It is up to you whether to use short selling as part of your investment plan.

But keep a few things in mind. First, many sophisticated portfolio managers use short selling. A big reason is to hedge a portfolio and allow for less volatile returns in an overall portfolio.

Next, short selling is a natural part of any sophisticated market. When the first markets started in the 1600s, it was not long until short selling emerged.

True, there can be manipulation and fraud with short selling. But this is not an argument to prohibit short selling. After all, investors who buy stocks can also engage in manipulation and fraud.

Top academics have studied short selling and have concluded that the process brings stability to markets. It can help prevent bubbles and bring realism to stock prices. According to Arturo Bris, William Goetzmann, and Ning Zhu (of the Yale School of Management):

> "…[M]arkets exist to facilitate the efficient pricing of assets, and that restricting short-sales reduces market efficiency."

In the end, knowledge is power—especially for investing. Short selling is often overlooked, but, in this book, we provide the essentials you need to understand this classic investing tool.

CHAPTER 1

ESSENTIALS OF SHORT SELLING

While Wall Street has always been a center of controversy from time to time–scandals, quick-buck artists, manipulations—there has been one area that consistently has remained an object of scorn: short selling. Interestingly enough, this has been the case since the emergence of stock markets in the 1600s in the Dutch Republics.

When the tulip bulb bubble burst in the Dutch markets and many people lost their life savings, it certainly seemed like an injustice that there were others who were benefiting from the misfortune—that is, short sellers. Short sellers became pariahs. They also were blamed for the market collapse.

Since then, short sellers have been the object of scorn from the public and the subject of harsh regulations. Short selling, for example, was illegal in the United States until the 1850s. Then there was Napolean, who declared short selling "treason" because it prevented him from financing his wars. Even in recent times, there have been lashes at short sellers. For example, in 1995, the Finance Ministry of Malaysia proposed that short sellers be punished by caning.

IT'S DIFFERENT NOW

There was an attitude change after the burst of the bubble of 2000–2002. Short sellers were not necessarily seen as evil. In fact, it was short sellers who were the few to cast doubt on such companies as Enron, WorldCom, and Adelphia. Others who were paid lots of money for their work—such as analysts, investment bankers, and brokers–were still bullish and touting their stocks as prices went lower and lower.

Whether good or bad, today short selling is legal in the United States, and many investors engage in the activity. In fact, if you are an investor in a hedge fund, chances are the portfolio manager engages in short selling. Some mutual funds also engage in short selling.

Table 1.1 shows the number of shares short as of the end of January 2003.

As you can see, short selling is a common activity. Volumes of short shares certainly will change from year to year, but shorting will not go away. If anything, it is a natural part of any sophisticated financial system. Thus, it is smart for investors to understand the essentials of short selling.

WHAT IS SHORT SELLING?

The Securities and Exchange Commission (SEC) defines short selling as shown on the next page.

Table 1.1.   Short Shares

NAME	NUMBER OF SHARES SHORT (IN MILLIONS)
Microsoft	56.9
Home Depot	20.8
General Electric	38.4
Johnson & Johnson	27.6
Citigroup	34.3
Wal-Mart	40.1
IBM	30.8
Exxon	26.1

> . . . the sale of a security that the seller does not own or that the seller owns but does not deliver. In order to deliver the security to the purchaser, the short seller will borrow the security, typically from a broker-dealer or an institutional investor.

Although accurate, this is not a helpful definition. Basically, a short seller sells a stock he has borrowed (usually on margin) in hopes that the price drops so he can make a profit when he buys it back at a lower price. The short seller sells high and buys low, rather than buying low and then selling high (which is called going long).

To best understand short selling, let's take a look at an example. In this example, we'll show the six main steps of the process.

Step 1–Establish an Account: You need to open a brokerage account that allows for margin, as well as a minimum amount of cash or other securities. We discuss this in more detail in the next chapter.

Your account has $5000 in cash.

Step 2–Research the Company: You immerse yourself in the details of a company called ABC Inc. You realize that the company's growth is slowing down, yet the stock has not fallen as much as its industry peers. The current stock price is $20 per share. You think the stock can easily fall to $10.

Step 3–Initiate the Short Sell: You call your broker or click your online account to short 100 shares of ABC Inc. That is, your broker will sell 100 shares at $20 apiece and generate $2000 in gross proceeds.

Where do the 100 shares come from? After all, the buyer of the 100 shares will need to receive them! Can you sell something you do not own?

Step 4–Borrow the Shares: Because you do not own the 100 shares, you need to borrow them. The problem is there is no central market to lend and borrow shares.

Rather, your broker will first look at its firm's other client margin accounts. All margin agreements allow a broker to lend out shares. So if there are 100 shares in one of these accounts, you will be able to borrow them. The broker will then use a journal entry to carry out the transaction.

If there are no shares available from these accounts, the broker might then try to locate shares from other institutions. If this fails, then you simply will not be able to short the 100 shares. In Wall Street parlance, you were unable to get "the borrow."

As a general rule, large stocks are typically easy to borrow. Small, thinly traded stocks, on the other hand, can be difficult if not impossible to borrow.

Step 5–Selling the Shares: Your broker was able to obtain 100 shares from a client account, whose name is Jane. The broker sells the 100 shares for $2000 and this amount is held in an escrow.

Step 6–Covering the Short Position: You were right. The stock price collapsed to $10 per share. You decide to take your profits and cover your short position. That is, you instruct your broker to buy 100 shares of ABC Inc. for $1000 and then the broker delivers the 100 shares back to Jane. You then collect the $2000 and have a net profit of $1000.

Then again, if the stock increased, your profit would have turned into a loss. If the stock hit $30, you would cover the 100 shares for $3000 and keep the $2000, giving you a loss of $1000.

Essentially, short selling is really the reverse of the process of buying a stock long, as shown below:

Long Transaction	Buy now at a low price; sell later at a higher price
Short Transaction	Sell now at a high price; buy later at a lower price

THE WILD HISTORY OF SHORT SELLING

The history of short selling is full of flamboyant characters and incredible feats of market manipulation. As is the case with any time in history, there are many greedy investors—whether long or short.

One of the oldest manipulations for short sellers is the *corner*. Let's say a wily investor, John, knows that there are several

---

WHO WAS THE FIRST SHORT SELLER?

It's impossible to know the answer to this question. But the first well-known short seller was Isaac Le Maire, who was a successful merchant. In the early 1600s, he began to short stocks on the Dutch stock exchange. One of his targets was the esteemed Dutch East India Company.

When the markets crashed in 1610, the Dutch authorities decided to outlaw short selling. The belief was that short selling was the responsible for the plunge.

---

short sellers who want to increase their short positions in XYZ Corp. John lends his shares to these short sellers, who then short the stock. John then aggressively purchases as many shares as possible of XYZ, which drives up the stock. The short sellers panic—but are unable to buy enough shares to cover their positions. In most cases, John would work out a settlement with the short sellers and take a hefty profit.

The corner was a popular technique during the 1800s and up to the late 1920s. Perhaps the most notorious short sellers were part of the "Robber Barons" of the 1800s. Regulation of the securities markets was practically nonexistent, and traders would do just about anything to make a buck. Even though short selling was banned until the 1850s, savvy traders still found ways to get around the rules.

During this era, railroad stocks were much like the Internet stocks of the 1990s. Volatility was incredible, and short sellers could make a fortune if they guessed right. But guesswork might not have been much of a factor; that is, traders would spread terrible rumors about companies to drive their stock prices down. In those days, some journalists were amenable to bribes.

However, it was typically the case that short sellers would get squeezed by a corner. One of the best practitioners was Daniel Drew, who was a street-smart investor and typically targeted railroads (his most notorious foray was for the Erie Railroad). His famous saying about the unfortunate short sellers who were caught in the vise of a corner: "He who sells what isn't his must buy it back or go to prison."

By the way, corners still happen occasionally in U.S. markets. An example was Chase Medical in 1988, in which two shareholders bought 109 percent of the float of the company's stock. The Securities and Exchange Commission brought suits against the two individuals.

REACTION TO EXCESS

The Roaring 1920s made some people extremely rich from the surge in stock prices. But when the markets crashed in 1929, the public lost confidence. It appeared that the financial markets were slanted to the rich and powerful. The individual investor would, in the end, suffer from the manipulations.

There were certainly many examples of questionable trading practices during the 1920s. William Durant, who founded General Motors, was also an aggressive stock trader. He formed large pools of money to corner stocks, such as International Nickel.

Then there was Albert Wiggin. He was president of Chase National Bank. In October 1929, he shorted 42,000 shares of his own company stock and made about $4 million on the transaction. Interestingly enough, Chase reimbursed him for his taxes.

When President Roosevelt came to power, he quickly passed wide-scale legislation to regulate the securities markets. The two main bills included the Securities Act of 1933 and the Securities Exchange Act of 1934. He established the Securities and Exchange Commission (SEC) to enforce the new securities laws and put Joseph Kennedy (the father of President John F. Kennedy) in charge. During the 1920s, Kennedy was known to have engaged in a variety of corners.

In the Securities Exchange Act of 1934, Section 10(a) provides for the SEC's powers to regulate short selling. We will cover these rules in Chapter 3. (By the way, it is now illegal for corporate insiders, like Wiggin, to short their own stock.)

LIVERMORE AND BARUCH

Two legendary short sellers in U.S. history are Jesse Livermore and Bernard Baruch. As the stock markets got much bigger and more sophisticated, it became much more difficult to use market manipulations. Instead, short sellers had to use analysis to get their edge.

Livermore did not get a degree in finance; however, he did have an incredible intuition for numbers and finance. He could easily memorize the price histories of companies and could get a sense of the patterns almost instantly. In fact, it was this that helped establish the fundamentals of technical analysis.

His most notable short was the Union Pacific Railroad. A few months after taking his position, a massive earthquake hit San Francisco in October 1907. Livermore made about $3 million on the trade.

It did not take long for him to gain a reputation for being a top trader and his nickname was the "Boy Plunger." He even wrote a book, called *Reminiscences of a Stock Operator*, which is an investment classic.

Livermore was far from perfect. Several times, he went bust. But he always seemed to find a way to make back his fortune. Apparently, he netted about a $100 million when he shorted the stock market in 1929. When word of this spread, though, the public was in outrage and blamed him for the stock market crash. In 1940, Livermore committed suicide.

Then there is Baruch. Unlike Livermore, Baruch attended college and then worked at a variety of investment banks. He had a great analytical ability and made substantial amounts from his trading.

Perhaps his most memorable short sale was Amalgamated Copper. According to his analysis, he thought the copper market would soften—and it did. He made about $700,000 on the trade.

Over the years, Baruch wrote about his theories and strategies on short selling–which became the basis of his book, *Short Sales and the Manipulation of Securities* (1913). It was an attempt to try to prevent the U.S. government from imposing strenuous regulations on short selling. He thought short selling was very beneficial for the markets because it restrained speculation.

Ultimately, Baruch pursued a distinguished career in politics and became known as the "park bench statement" because of his advisory role for presidents Harding, Coolidge, and Hoover.

THE RISE OF INSTITUTIONS

The power of individual traders declined substantially after the 1920s. In its place came the rise of institutions. Mutual funds, pensions, and insurance companies became the major players in the securities markets.

However, these institutions did not directly engage in much short selling. Instead, this was the province of a new type of fund called the hedge fund (see Chapter 2 for a description of the structure).

One of the most successful hedge fund managers was George Soros. Born in Budapest in 1930, he emigrated to England to attend the London School of Economics. In 1956, he came to New York to start his hedge fund.

He did not distinguish between long or short. Rather, he pursued whatever transaction would net his fund the most money. When the markets were heavily bearish in the 1970s, he was able to generate significant returns because of his wise short sales. He would look at major trends and spot the most vulnerable companies. One was Avon, which he shorted at $120 and covered at $20.

DECADE OF GREED

With the bull market of the 1980s, it was more difficult for short sellers to make money—but this didn't stop some from trying. It was during this time that a new type of hedge fund emerged: the short-only fund.

One that garnered much fanfare was a fund managed by the Feschbach brothers: Matt, Kurt, and Joe. They were unabashed bears and constantly looked for companies that were hopefully frauds. This meant incredible analysis of the financials, as well as interviewing competitors, suppliers, and just about anybody that could shed light on a company's shenanigans.

A big trade was ZZZZ Best, a company founded by a super-salesman teenager Barry Minkow. The firm specialized in carpet cleaning. When ZZZZ Best announced multimillion contracts, the Feschbach brothers were instantly skeptical. After some spade work, they realized that it was impossible to charge such prices. So they shorted the stock.

Eventually, ZZZZ Best plunged into bankruptcy after it was discovered that the books were being cooked.

By the 1990s, the Feschbach brothers closed their fund. Simply put, it was too difficult for them to find short sale candidates. The markets were too bullish.

It wasn't until 2000 that short-only funds started to make a comeback. One of the top was Kynikos Associates, which is run by James Chanos (we look at more detail of this fund in Chapter 2).

CONCLUSION

In this chapter, we have provided a flavor of the short sale game. It is not a particularly easy technique. Even top traders have problems—especially when markets surge. But, for the most part, it is the top investors that find a balance between long and short strategies. This is what Soros did, and it meant incredible returns for his investors. In the next chapter, we look at the main reasons to consider the practice of short selling.

CHAPTER 2

WHY BECOME
A SHORT SELLER?

As you read this book, it would be normal to ask yourself: "Why would I ever engage in short selling? The risks are so high." It is absolutely true that there are many risks to short selling—but this is the case with any investment technique. However, investment theory indicates that, within a diversified portfolio, high-risk activities can actually lower the overall risk level. It sounds kind of contradictory—but it is a crucial concept.

In this chapter, we look at an important reason to consider short selling: asset allocation. We also look at other reasons, such as avoiding buying bad stocks and improving your abilities in terms of stock analysis.

ASSET ALLOCATION

Asset allocation is a highly complex subject. There is a tremendous amount of academic research about it, and many financial planners spend much of their time refining the concepts. Despite this, you do not need to be a Ph.D. in finance to use the principles of asset allocation.

The underlying foundation of asset allocation is the following: You invest in a variety of asset classes, such as stocks (small, mid, and large cap), bonds, precious metals, international markets, and cash. If one investment falls, another investment will hopefully succeed. This helps to even-out the volatility in the overall portfolio; risk should be reduced.

Interestingly enough, studies show that 90 percent of the return derived from a portfolio comes from the mix of the asset classes. The other 10 percent comes from what particular investments you choose.

This is not to say that asset allocation is mandatory. During the 1990s, many investors concentrated their portfolios on tech stocks. When the markets boomed, this was certainly a very wise choice. Then again, assuming investors did not sell their huge gains, they wound up losing much as the technology sector plunged.

Take comfort in knowing that the roots of asset allocation come from a very smart University of Chicago finance professor, Harold Markowitz. During the 1950s, he spent much time looking at ways to measure the risk of a portfolio—which was revolutionary at the time. Just like any pioneering work, he had the help of many other smart people, such as William Sharpe. In the end, Markowitz fashioned modern portfolio theory (ie, asset allocation) and won the Nobel Prize for Economics for his efforts.

By combining asset classes, asset allocation can help increase returns while reducing the overall risk level. It should be no surprise that many institutional investment portfolios—pensions, mutual funds, insurance companies—rely on asset allocation.

DEVELOPING AN ASSET ALLOCATION PROGRAM

How much should you put in stocks or bonds or cash or other investments? First, you can get the help of a financial planner. Make sure the planner has sophisticated software and charges on an hourly basis, not on the commissions generated from certain types of investments.

Next, there are many online calculators that can help you develop your asset allocation:

www.quicken.com

www.smartmoney.com

www.money.com

Figure 2.1 is an asset allocation chart from *Money.com*:

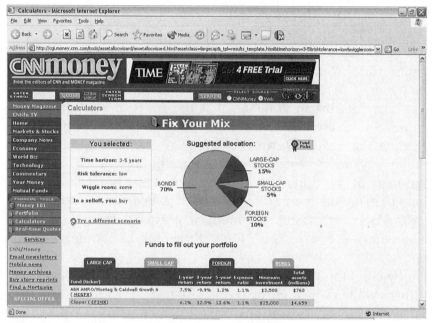

FIGURE 2.1.   At *Money.com*, you can easily set up an asset allocation strategy.

To determine the allocation, the asset allocator asks about your risk tolerance, as well as your financial goals.

While these calculators are very useful, there is a problem: Most of them focus on what investments to *buy*. The problem is: Suppose all the asset classes fall? In this scenario, the diversification does not protect your portfolio.

A better approach is to hedge a portion of the portfolio, which is done by selling short. So if the long portion is experiencing problems, part of this should be offset by a rise on the short portion.

You could, for instance, allocate about 10 percent to 15 percent of your portfolio in hedged investments. This could represent:

- Short selling of individual stocks (which we will explain throughout this book)
- Hedge funds (see sidebar)

Perhaps, as you get more concerned about the overall market, you can boost the percentage of the short allocation. Or if you think the markets look undervalued, you can do the reverse.

Keep in mind another strategy: rebalancing. Over time, you might need to revaluate the allocations because of changes in valuations. If the stock market has surged, this might mean that the stock portion of your asset allocation is overweighed. You can reduce exposure in stocks and move the money into other areas that have shrunk.

BETTER ANALYSIS

Even if you do not short sell individual stocks, it is still important to understand the process of short selling. A top short seller who teaches an MBA course on investments says that when he presents a case study to his students, he says: "Do intensive analysis. If you like the stock, recommend that we buy it. If you don't like the stock, recommend that we short it. All great investors look at any investment in this manner."

In other words, great investors always look for the downsides—which is what short sellers constantly do for a living. In fact, the life of a pure short seller is not easy. There are a variety of regulations that restrain short selling and, of course, society is not enamored with them (it is rare to see a short seller brag about his profession at a cocktail party).

Also, the general trend for stocks, throughout history, is for them to increase in value. Again, this is bad news for short sellers. In some cases, the markets can surge to irrational levels. It should be no surprise that many short sellers left their profession during the roaring bull market of the 1990s.

Basically, a successful short seller needs to do extensive analysis. They analyze the financials; they study the industry

THE BASICS OF HEDGE FUNDS

In 1949, the academic and former editor of *Fortune* magazine, Alfred Jones, started the first hedge fund. He believed that it was impossible to predict the direction of the market and thought that finding ways to neutralize the effects of market swings— through buying long and shorting—was the best policy.

His other insight was to raise money only from wealthy individuals and institutions. This meant he did not have to register his fund with the cumbersome federal securities regulations. It also meant he could pursue his alternative investment strategies because these investors were considered to be "sophisticated."

In terms of compensation, he took a 1-percent fee for money under management. Then, he got 20 percent of any of the profits from his performance.

How was his performance? It was phenomenal over the years and, no doubt, attracted much attention. Other great investors, such as George Soros, formed their own hedge funds.

How has the structure of hedge funds changed? Not much. They still are very similar to what Jones created in 1949.

But with the popularity of hedge funds, it is now becoming easier for individuals to participate. For example, some funds have minimum investment requirements of $25,000. These are typically known as hedge fund of funds. As the name implies, these are hedge funds that invest in other hedge funds—so individual investors can help spread their risk.

Be wary: There are many hedge funds. In some cases, the portfolio managers have very little experience or might be even downright frauds. Because of the lower disclosure requirements, it is easier to hide wrongdoing with a hedge fund.

Just like any form of investment, make sure you do your homework before you sign over a check.

trends; they listen to conference calls; they track competitive forces.

To understand the process, let's take a look at one of the top short sellers, James Chanos. In 1985, he founded his own short-only hedge fund called Kynikos. He has seven people on his staff and manages more than $1 billion in client assets. It is the largest short-only firm in the world.

Chanos got his start in investments as a securities analyst at a small investment bank 1980. Before this, he graduated from Yale with a B.A. in Economics and Political Science.

Chanos follows this process when finding short sale candidates: companies that appear to have

- materially overstated earnings
- been victims of a flawed business plan
- been engaged in outright fraud

One of his most memorable short sales first came to light in October 2000, when he read a local edition of the *Wall Street Journal* that cast doubt on the accounting of Enron. The accounting method was called "gain-on-sale," and Chanos understood this to be an aggressive way to report profits as management could easily adjust assumptions to inflate the numbers.

Next, he downloaded Enron's financial statements from EDGAR, the electronic system for securities documents. In the 10-K filing, he realized that despite the aggressive accounting, Enron's return on capital was a very small 7 percent. Yet Wall Street was valuing the company as if it had a much higher return on capital.

Other concerns:

- A disclosure indicating that an executive was a principal in a firm dealing with Enron. But the language was extremely vague.
- Large amounts of insider selling of Enron stock.
- The company's initiatives into the broadband industry, even though it was beginning to collapse.

A month later, Chanos's firm started to short the stock. Of course, he made a bundle.

AVOIDING BAD STOCKS

If you had several dot-coms that went to zero in a few years, it would have had a discernable impact on your portfolio, even if you practiced asset allocation. A few bad stocks can mean trouble.

If you are afraid of short selling, the analytical techniques of a good short seller will help to avoid horrendous stock picks.

CONCLUSION

When setting up your asset allocation, it is important to realize that it is far from a scientific process. Yet, when the computer generates specific advice and exact percentages, asset allocation might look like it is very precise and incontrovertible.

Instead, asset allocation is ultimately about your goals and tolerance for risk. If your goals are long-term (more than five years) and your risk level is high, then you can be aggressive. If not, it is a good idea to tone down your portfolio, which typically means shifting money from stocks to bonds and cash.

In this next chapter, we look at the mechanics of margin accounts.

CHAPTER 3

YOU NEED A MARGIN ACCOUNT

Several years ago, I opened a brokerage account to engage in short selling. My new broker was definitely skeptical. "You must first open a margin account," he told me. "I'm supposed to give you a disclaimer. Basically, I will tell you that a margin account is like crack. It's addictive. And it kills."

This was good advice. Margin is not for the casual investor (nor is short selling, for that matter). There are many examples of investors who lost a tremendous amount of money because of margin accounts. In fact, a major reason for the crash of 1929 was the tremendous amount of margin borrowing.

In this chapter, we look at the key dynamics of margin accounts and how they relate to short selling. Keep in mind that this is a complex area and we are only looking at the surface features. There are margin specialists at brokerage firms that know the nuances.

In other words, if you have a question about a margin account, feel free to ask. Your broker might not know the answer—but the margin specialist should. Asking lots of questions will go a long way to understanding the process.

TYPES OF ACCOUNTS

There are two types of brokerage accounts: cash and margin. The cash account is the simplest type and means that, to buy a security, you need to have the cash to make the purchase. A margin account, on the other hand, allows you to borrow money using cash and securities as collateral.

In order to short sell stocks, you need to first establish a margin account with a brokerage firm. There is no way around this; it is the law established during the Great Depression and is called Regulation T.

As with any borrowing, it is not free. There is an interest rate for the loan, although the rate is typically low compared to other rates, especially credit card rates. Moreover, the higher the amount borrowed, the lower the interest rate.

Table 3.1 shows what the loan rates were for Schwab on February 15, 2003.

Margin provides a variety of benefits to investors. First, it allows for convenience. For instance, if you want to buy 100 shares but do not have immediate cash to make the transaction, you can borrow the funds against the value of your account.

Actually, there is no requirement that you must buy securities with margin. You can use the loan for a car or a boat or even a house. Depending on the account, it is as simple as writing a check or using a credit card.

Table 3.1 Margin Rates for Schwab Customers

AMOUNT BORROWED	RATE
$0-$9,999.99	7.75%
$10,000-$24,999.99	6.75%
$25,000-$49,999.99	6.25%
$50,000-$99,999.99	5.25%
$100,000-$249,999.99	5.125%
$250,000-$999,999.99	5.00%
$1,000,000+	4.75%

FILLING OUT THE FORM

The account form for a margin account can be quite daunting (it is really meant to be that way—so you do not read it). Read the margin account before signing. Unfortunately, you will find a lot of legalese.

As a guide, here are some factors to look for:

Background Information: You will need to specify your income, net worth, and employment status. Be accurate. If there is a dispute, a brokerage firm can use any false information to bolster their case.

Investment Experience: The account form will ask for information regarding experience with investments, as well as your objectives. Again, be truthful. If you say that your goal is for "speculative" investments, then your brokerage firm will have an easier defense if there is a future dispute.

Insider Status: You need to specify if you are an insider of a public company (that is, director or officer or major shareholder—usually 10 percent or more of any class of stock). The reason is that an insider is prohibited from shorting their own stock.

Credit Check: Usually, a margin account will allow the brokerage firm to conduct a credit check on you. If you are denied a margin account because of a credit check, you have the right to request a copy of the report. It is not uncommon for these reports to have false information.

Insurance: All brokerage firms belong to the Securities Investor Protection Corporation (SIPC). This organization protects client accounts in the event of a brokerage failure. Both long and short investments are covered by the SIPC. The minimum amount insured is $500,000, with no more than $100,000 of this in cash. Example: Suppose you have an account of $150,000 in cash, $300,000 in long positions, and $100,000 in short positions. If the brokerage goes bust, you will get your $300,000 in long and $100,000 in short positions. But you will only get $100,000 in cash. However, many brokerage firms will buy insurance that includes amounts much higher than the minimum. E*TRADE provides up to $49.5 million in protection, of which $900,000 is in cash.

Closing Your Account: You can do this at any time. But if there are any outstanding short positions, you must close all of them.

Street Name: You are required to keep all securities in a margin account in *street name*. That is, your brokerage will have physical control of the stock certificates. This does not mean the brokerage owns the stock; instead, you still have beneficial ownership. Actually, having certificates in street name is a smart thing to do. It provides for SIPC protection, allows you to get updates (annual reports, proxies, etc), and gives you the ability to use limit and stop orders. If you do not have a security in street name, it can be a time-consuming process if you lose the certificate.

Hypothecation: This is the fancy way of saying that you allow your brokerage firm to lend your securities. This helps facilitate short selling activity.

Rehypothecation: This allows a brokerage firm to get loans based on securities in your margin account.

Interest: You agree to pay an interest rate that varies over time.

WHAT IS MARGINABLE?

Your broker will tell you what is marginable. The following are marginable:

- Treasury bonds, corporate bonds, municipal bonds, and government agency bonds

- Stocks on the New York Stock Exchange that trade over $3 per share

- Most stocks that trade over $4 per share on the NASDAQ

- Most mutual funds, so long as held for at least 30 days

The following are not marginable:

- UGMA and UTMA accounts

- Options

- Annuities

- Precious metals

- Money market funds

- Certificates of deposit

After you sign the margin agreement, your broker will look to see what securities in your account are *marginable*. After all, a lightly traded stock might not be eligible, but certainly a stock like Cisco or IBM would.

The broker will then indicate to you what the *borrowing power* of the account is. So long as you meet certain requirements, you can take loans against your account at any time.

The Federal Reserve sets the minimum allowed that can be borrowed in a margin account, which is 50 percent of the value of the marginable stocks. The Fed can change this rate at anytime—but this is a rare occurrence.

Keep in mind, though, that the stock exchanges and your brokerage firm can increase these requirements.

Let's take a look at a margin transaction:

You think XYZ will zoom in value. The stock price is $20 and you have $2000 in cash. So you can buy 100 shares. Suppose the stock doubles and you sell all your shares. Your profit will be $2000.

If you use margin, you can use the following equation to determine how many shares of XYZ you can buy:

Value in the account/margin requirement

$$\$2,000/0.50 = \$4,000$$

In other words, you can buy 200 shares. Again, if XYZ doubled in price to $40, the value of your account will be $8000. After you repay the $2000 loan, you will have cleared a $4000 profit or a 200-percent rate of return on the initial $2000 investment of cash (see Table 3.2). As with any type of borrowing, you can take advantage of the concept of leverage. With our example, for every 10-percent increase in investment, your rate of return is leveraged by 20 percent. Table 3.2 shows the difference between a $2000 account that is margined and non-margined.

Assume that you do not sell the stock in your margin account. Currently, the value is $8000 and the loan is $2000. But the loan only represents 25 percent of the total value of the account. Can you now borrow more money? Yes you can. The more equity that builds in the account, the more you can borrow.

Table 3.2   Magnifying Returns with Margin

	WITHOUT MARGIN	WITH MARGIN
Initial investment	$2,000	$2,000
Amount borrowed	$0	$2,000
Stock purchased	$2,000	$4,000
Stock value after doubling	$4,000	$8,000
Profit	$2,000	$4,000
Rate of return	100%	200%

To determine the additional amount, take these three steps:

Step 1: The total amount of the account is $8000.

Step 2: Subtract the $2000 loan, which equals $6000.

Step 3: You can borrow an additional $6000 and buy even more stock.

Of course, leverage has a downside. Just like any borrowing, if done without prudence, the results can be disastrous. During the 1920s, the margin requirements for margin accounts were very lax—typically about 10 percent or so. This helped fuel a tremendous bull market. Unfortunately, when the markets crashed, many investors were wiped out, as the value of their accounts plunged below the amount they owed.

With our XYZ example, let's say the stock price falls to $1 per share. In this case, the value of the account is $200, on which you invested $2000. Also, you still owed $2000. In all, your losses are $3800.

Before this happens, a brokerage firm will take precautions. This is in the form of *maintenance calls*. The definition is: The market value of your margined securities—subtracted from the amount borrowed, which is also known as the *debit balance*—falls below a certain percentage threshold. If this is triggered, the brokerage will require that you deposit more cash or securities into the account. This is known as a *margin call*. If you do not do this or are unable to, then the brokerage has the right to sell any securities to meet the maintenance calls.

Generally, a brokerage firm will notify you about a margin call, but this is not required. A brokerage firm has the right to sell any of the securities in your account to meet a margin call without your consent. There is also no right for an extension on a margin call. But it is still worth asking for one if you are having difficulties.

SHORT SELLING AND MARGIN ACCOUNTS

Whether you use a margin account to either buy or short a stock, the main principles apply. That is, there is an initial margin requirement and a maintenance requirement. Moreover, if the account value increases, the borrowing power will increase. If the account falls in value and falls below the maintenance requirement, a margin call is issued.

But there are some real differences between handling long and short transactions in a margin account. In light of this, many brokerage firms segregate the activities to make record keeping easier. If is often said that short positions are in a subaccount of a margin account, for instance.

One key difference is in the level of the maintenance requirement. For long positions, it is usually 30 percent. A short position, on the other hand, might be about 35 percent.

To understand a short sale transaction within a margin account, let's take an example. You have a margin account with $5,000 in cash. You decide to short 100 shares of XYZ at $100 each. The chart would look like the following:

Proceeds	$10,000
Cash	$5,000
Total	$15,000
Cost to close the short sale	$10,000
Equity in the account	$5,000

The proceeds of $10,000 is also known as the credit balance. You are not allowed to take this from the account—that is, until you close out the short position. You do not even earn interest on this amount. Good deal for the brokerage? Definitely. We will explore this in more detail in Chapter 4, "The Costs and Dangers of Short Selling"

The cash is 50 percent of the credit balance, which means that the account is in accordance with Reg. T. Let's say that your short position does not go so well, as the stock price increases to $130. The new chart is:

Proceeds	$10,000
Cash	$5,000
Total	$15,000
Cost to close the short sale	$13,000
Equity in the account	$2,000

The price rise decreases the equity in the account ($15,000 total minus the cost to short, $13,000) to $2000. The equity as a percentage of the cost to close is:

$$\$2000/\$13,000 = 15\%$$

This is far below the 35 percent maintenance requirement. Unless you put more cash or securities in the account, you will receive a margin call.

SPECIAL DAY TRADING RULES

In response to newcomers engaging in day trading, the self-regulatory agency for the securities industry, the National Association of Securities Dealers (NASD), passed some new regulations. If you are classified as a day trader, there is a requirement to have a minimum of $25,000 in your account.

The main rule is that a day trader is someone who executes four or more day-trades within five business days (a day trade is a long or short transaction that lasts less than a trading day).

STOCK MARKETS

There are many places you can transact short sales. These exchanges include:

New York Stock Exchange (NYSE): This was founded in 1792 and is the oldest stock exchange in the United States. While the exchange has spent billions of dollars on computer systems, the general approach to buying and selling stocks is the same when it started: open auction. There are roughly 2800 companies listed on the exchange, and each company has at least one specialist. The specialist makes a market in the stock. That is, if someone wants to buy stock and there is no seller, then the specialist will step in to make the trade.

American Stock Exchange (AMEX): This exchange also uses the open auction system. Whereas the NYSE handles major companies—such as IBM and GE—the AMEX focuses on smaller issues. The AMEX also has a thriving market in stock options.

NASDAQ (National Association of Securities Dealers Automated Quotation System): The NASDAQ is the result of the computer age. Founded in 1971, this was set up as a computer and telecommunications network that handles the buying and selling of stock. There is no central trading floor like the NYSE and AMEX.

To allow for liquidity, the NASDAQ has a participant similar to a specialist: the market maker.

Over the Counter (OTC) Bulletin Board: This is a quotation service geared for small companies. The volume is usually very light, and fraud can be a problem. So it is no surprise that short sellers can find opportunities in this marketplace. But, because of the light volume, it can be difficult to borrow shares to execute a short sale transaction.

CONCLUSION

Before we leave this chapter and discuss the costs and dangers of short selling in the next chapter, it is important to underscore the importance of being cautious with margin accounts. With these accounts, it is easy to go too far and, if things go against you, the account value can rapidly evaporate.

The best approach is to start slowly—and build your knowledge over time. All good short sellers have had to do this. In the end, it can save you from lots of trouble.

CHAPTER 4

THE COSTS AND DANGERS OF SHORT SELLING

Short selling is a very profitable activity for brokerage firms. It is investors who provide the nice profits to brokerage firms.

Perhaps the main reasons ordinary investors pay high fees is that they do not understand the complex process of a short sale transaction. A broker can easily hide many fees along the way. Then again, sophisticated investors—such as hedge funds—understand this process and are able to negotiate better rates on their trades.

This chapter will look at the main costs of short selling:

- Bid/Ask Spread
- Margin Interest
- Commission

Besides hidden costs, there are also a variety of dangers and restrictions that you must be aware of. We will also look at these, which include:

- Uptick Rule
- Unlimited Losses
- Buy-in and Short Squeeze

BID AND ASK SPREAD

When you look at a stock quote, you will notice two prices: the bid and the ask. Here's an example from Microsoft:

Close	Change	Bid	Ask
26.04	+0.11	25.95	26.05

In a short sale, the ordinary investor will sell the stock at the bid. The ordinary investor's broker will transmit this order to the stock exchange. There, a specialist or market maker will carry out the sale and take a profit based on the difference between the bid and the ask—which is known as the *spread*.

For Microsoft, the market maker would get a 10-cent spread. This would be a tight spread because there is a small difference between the bid and the ask price. While the profits on each trade might be small, the market makers and specialists make money from large volumes of trading.

For stocks that do not trade much, the opposite is the case. To compensate for the low volume, there will be a bigger spread.

The spread is a cost the ordinary investor must ultimately pay for. Unfortunately, many investors do not realize this and use market orders when placing trades. This puts the investor at the mercy of the market, and you are likely not to get a good price on your trades.

The solution? Use limit orders. This is easy to do with any online broker firm (or with your full-service broker). With a limit order, you are establishing the price you want to make the trade at.

MARGIN INTEREST

Many firms will charge you interest on the value of the securities shorted in your account. With low interest rates, this might not seem like a lot—but it can add up over time.

If you shorted $10,000 in XYZ and the interest charges on your account are 6 percent, then you will pay $600 in fees for the year.

Institutional investors typically do not pay these interest costs. The exception would be if a stock is small or hard to borrow.

If you decide to short a stock—which is fairly liquid in terms of trading volume—request that your broker not charge the margin interest. If this is rejected, then say you will take your account somewhere else.

COMMISSIONS

Commissions vary greatly between full-service and discount brokerage firms. You pay higher commissions to a full-service brokerage because of the personal advice and counsel you receive. This can certainly be helpful if you are interested in financial planning advice. However, in many cases, a broker is not very knowledgeable about short selling. In fact, it is often the case that brokerage firms frown upon brokers building a short-selling business.

Besides, the research services of a brokerage firm tends to have a bias for opportunities to buy stocks, not short them.

Given the above, it typically makes the most sense to use a discount broker when handling your short sales.

THE UPTICK RULE

What if you could not buy a stock when it fell? That would make it difficult to trade, right? Of course.

But a similar situation exists for short selling, and it is called the uptick rule. It was during the Depression that this rule was introduced. The perception was that short sellers aggravated the fall in the stock markets. The solution was to not allow short sellers to short a stock that is falling in price.

This rule is still in effect today and definitely makes it difficult for short sellers to make their transactions.

The Securities and Exchange Commission has conducted three studies on the rule (from 1963 to 1991) and has concluded that short sellers often do not have much power on overall stock prices and that the uptick rule did not necessarily protect investors.

In 1999, the SEC published a Concept Statement to get comments from the industry and attempt to undo the uptick rule. You can find more information about this at: *http://www.sec.gov/rules/concept/34-42037.htm*. However, so far, there appears little movement to change the rule. Expect this to be a part of short selling for the foreseeable future.

UNLIMITED LOSSES

If you short 100 shares at $10 each, the maximum profit you can make is $1,000. This would happen if the stock goes to zero. How much can you lose? The typically answer is "unlimited losses." This is not an accurate phrase since stocks cannot increase to infinity (and, if they did, you probably do not have infinite capital to meet your margin calls).

But a stock can easily increase 100 percent or more in a short period of time. In other words, you can lose much more than you can gain when you short a stock.

DISCIPLINE IS CRUCIAL

How can you use discipline in your short selling? Ultimately, this depends on the person. But here's an example from a top short seller: If he generates a profit of 25 percent to 30 percent, he will close out his position. Also, he does not want to hold a position for more than three months, because of the interest costs. Also, if his position generates a loss of 20 percent to 25 percent, he automatically closes the transaction.

That is why you need to employ strong discipline when shorting. Unfortunately, there are many examples of investors who did not practice discipline. One person I know, for instance, decided to short *Amazon.com*. He committed $25,000 to the trade. Within a few hours, he got a margin call. He was convinced about his analysis and used $50,000 to meet the margin call and short even more stock. By the end of the day, he lost everything and was broke. And, yes, within a month, the stock price did decline.

THE BUY-IN AND THE SHORT SQUEEZE

Let's say you short a stock at $50 per share. A day later, it surges to $55. You think this is a short-term blip and will hold on to your position.

Then you receive a notice from your broker: You must unwind your short position.

The reason? There was a "buy-in." When you sign a margin agreement, you agree to allow your broker to essentially force you to cover your short at any time.

A broker does not want to harm a client relationship and will try not to trigger a buy-in, but there might be no choice. A buy-in is the result of a stock that becomes hard to borrow. In our example, when the stock went from $50 to $55, there were some investors who took profits. These investors had margin accounts, which is where you got your shares to short. When these investors sold their stock, the broker needed to locate shares to carry out the transactions. Since it was difficult to locate more shares, the broker called your position.

This process often creates a "short squeeze." As a stock price increases, there are more buy-ins, which increases the stock price even more. Also, other short sellers might get scared and close out their positions, which adds more fuel to the stock price. To help avoid a short squeeze, you can use the following strategies:

- Avoid Hard-to-Borrow Stocks: Ask your broker if the stock you are shorting is hard to borrow.

- Short-Interest Ratio: This is a popular calculation for measuring the amount of short selling in a stock. The equation is:

Short Interest/Average Daily Volume

If a stock has short interest of 2 million shares and only trades 200,000 shares a day, it will take approximately 10 days of current volume to unwind the short position. As a general rule, if the short interest ratio is more than a week, the stock could be vulnerable to a short squeeze.

CONCLUSION

No doubt, short selling can be scary. As you can see, there are many things that can go wrong when you short a stock. This

---

CAN SHORT SELLERS SUE COMPANIES?

Shareholders have the right to sue public companies if there is fraud on the markets, such as misleading statements or outright lies. These actions are known as derivative lawsuits and have exploded during the bear markets of 2000-2002.

If a company does commit a fraud, can a short seller sue a company? The answer is "no." The reason is that a short seller does not own any stock, and so cannot file a derivative suit.

Companies have, though, filed suits against short sellers. One of the charges is defamation. That is, a company is accusing a short selling for making false claims about the company for the sole purpose of driving down the stock price.

These cases can be quite expensive and time-consuming.

In some instances, a company will file a suit against a person making negative posts on a discussion board—especially if they have a loyal following. So it is a good idea to avoid altogether making negative comments on the chart board or on any other public site if you have a short position in the stock.

does not mean you should avoid short selling. Actually, short selling is quite common.

As long as you understand the risks and use discipline, you should avoid many problems in your short selling activities.

In the next chapter, we look at the importance of timing and short selling.

C H A P T E R   5

TIMING IS EVERYTHING

In a criminal case, the prosecution must convince a jury "beyond a reasonable doubt" about the guilt of the accused. This is no easy task. Ideally, the prosecutor will have direct evidence of the crime—say, a videotape of a shooting.

But this is rare. In many cases, a prosecutor will have circumstantial evidence; that is, there are a variety of signs that the accused actually did commit the crime.

The same goes for short sellers. They expect not to find direct evidence (the proverbial "smoking gun") that a company is primed for a downward slide. The short seller expects that there will be red flags and danger signs that point to a potential short sale candidate.

Such evidence comes in two flavors for short sellers:

Danger Signs: This is something that clearly indicates a problem with a company. It could be an unexpected quarterly loss or the sudden resignation of the CEO and CFO.

The short seller often considers these danger signs to be a foreboding of more bad news to come. Then again, this might not happen. Perhaps it was a one-time event and the company is actually very solid.

This is why the stock price typically does not plunge on danger signs. It is also why it is a risky practice for short sellers to base their decisions on danger signs.

Trigger Events: This is bad news that does have an adverse impact on the stock price. A short seller will likely pounce on this information and accumulate a short position. The belief is based on the "cockroach theory." That is, the events are likely to get worse and worse. So there is more downside for short sellers to profit from.

Let's now take a look at the danger signs and trigger events that short sellers focus on.

DANGER SIGN 1: FADS

A fad is a high-growth business that suddenly evaporates. Consumers tire of the product and move onto something else.

The tough part for a short seller is distinguishing a fad from a real business. For example, at first, fast food looked like a fad. But McDonald's kept growing and proving the skeptics wrong. Or, take a look at Starbucks. At some point, customers would not want to buy expensive coffee, right? So far, it appears Starbucks is not a fad but a sustainable business.

Despite this, there are three areas that are prone to fads:

Restaurants: Successes like McDonald's and Starbucks are rare. In fact, many restaurants are really fads. This is especially the case with theme restaurants, like Planet Hollywood. There was also the bagel mania of the mid 1990s, which saw most of these companies eventually go bust.

Toys: Some toys can span generations, such as Barbie. But many toys quickly flame out, as children are extremely fickle. Examples include Coleco's Cabbage Patch dolls and Happiness Express's Mighty Morphin Power Rangers.

Technology: A technology product can grow at high rates. The problem is that it is difficult for a company to come out with a new version of the product. By that time, competitors have flooded the market with alternatives.

This happened with the former leader in handheld devices, Palm. After its tremendous success, many other companies came into the market (Microsoft, Handspring, Sony, and Hewlett-Packard).

DANGER SIGN 2:
NO MORE BIG GROWTH

All companies have limits. At some point, a company runs out of markets to sell its goods, and the growth rate moderates. Short sellers like these types of companies, especially if analysts and investors still think the high growth rates will continue.

Some short sellers look for the "$20 billion curse." The theory is that, when a company hits $20 billion in sales, the growth rate will slow down. For example, to grow the company at 20 percent would mean increase sales by a whopping $4 billion.

DANGER SIGN 3:
INTENSIFIYING COMPETITION

Competition is definitely good for consumers. It ultimately means more selection, better prices, and better quality. But competition is a scary thing for companies that want to maintain their edge.

Short sellers look for fast-growing companies that do not have a way to protect their product (such as through a patent). At some point, competitors will enter the marketplace to take advantage of the abnormal profits.

Signs to look for in rising competition include:

- Discounting
- Lawsuits against competitors
- Calling for government action against competitors
- Several quarters of less-than-expected earnings growth

DANGER SIGN 4:
FLAWED BUSINESS MODEL

A short seller will spend much time analyzing a company's business model. Will the model make money? What makes it unique? If a short seller cannot answer these questions, then he might have a good short sale prospect.

During the dot-com mania, there were clearly many businesses that lacked viable business models. Then again, there are also many nontech companies that suffer the same fate (as seen above, the theme restaurants appear to have problems with their business model).

Another thing short sellers look at is when a business model changes from year to year. If a business model is sustainable and solid, it should be lasting.

DANGER SIGN 5:
MANAGEMENT PROBLEMS

Short sellers do a background check on the management team. This is done by looking at the company's Web site and proxy statements. You can also do Web searches at *www.google.com*.

Problem areas include: prior bankruptcies (especially personal bankruptcies); reprimands or sanctions from governmental authorities; and lack of experience in the industry.

DANGER SIGN 6:
HYPE

A company wants to look good to the public and shareholders. It means a better stock price.

Unfortunately, some companies go beyond good PR and delve into downright hype and even lies.

A short seller will be alerted to:

- A company publishes several press releases every day.
- The company's press releases use hyperbole. Example: "our product is revolutionary."
- The company's CEO seems to be mostly doing interviews, not running the business.

DANGER SIGN 7:
SKEPTICISM FROM THE PUBLIC

Many short sellers will engage in "tire kicking." This means talking to customers and suppliers. Is the product really good? Or are there problems?

Professional short sellers have the means to do this kind of analysis.

But can you, as an individual investor, do the same thing? Yes, it is possible. But it can be done in an indirect way. One way is to network with knowledgeable people in the industry.

Example: An investor was interested in shorting the stock of VISX, a pioneer in LASIK surgery. Unless you were a doctor, it was probably difficult to evaluate this possible transaction. But why not ask a doctor who is currently using the system? In fact, the investor did and learned that the doctor was ready to purchase a better system—from another company.

Other ways to do tire kicking include:

Local Newspapers: Reporters at local newspapers often get stories before the national press. This how famed short seller James Chanos was alerted to the problems at Enron. He read the local edition of *The Wall Street Journal*.

Discussion Boards: These can be areas full of hype and even juvenile antics. But sometimes you can get real nuggets of information. Or you might find a link to a good article.

The top discussion boards include:

MotleyFool.com

Ragingbull.com

Siliconinvestor.com

Yahoo.com

Industry Conferences: These are often free. You can get lots of information about different companies, as well as network with experts in the industry.

Let's now take a look at trigger events:

TRIGGER EVENT 1:
FALL IN PRICE

A company can maintain a high stock value even as danger signs continue to accumulate. This was the case with Enron, WorldCom, and other major flameouts.

But at some point, investors begin to lose confidence and sell their stock holdings. Many short sellers wait for this to happen. To them, it is a vindication of the danger points that have been accumulating, as well as a harbinger of more bad news to come.

A short seller will want at least two danger points and a sudden drop in a stock price of at least 25 percent to indicate an entry point for a short sale.

TRIGGER EVENT 2:
RESIGNATIONS

Short sellers want to see unexpected resignations of the CEO or the CFO (preferably, both). The officer will likely say they are leaving to pursue other opportunities or that they want to attend to personal issues. But investors will scratch their heads and wonder: If the company is doing so well, why leave? After all, many CEOs want to continue earning their salary—and enjoy the bonuses and stock options—as well as build a legacy to be proud of.

Short sellers are even happier when there are no replacements for the CEO or CFO. This is an indication that there are serious problems with the company. Perhaps the board discovered major problems and requested immediate resignation.

It is also an alert to short sellers when a company's auditor resigns. If it is over a dispute of accounting, then this is very encouraging for short sellers (the reason for the resignation must be disclosed to the public).

TRIGGER EVENT 3:
TRADING HALTS AND SUSPENSIONS

Investors often confuse trading halts with trading suspensions. But there is a significant difference.

A trading halt is the action of a stock exchange to temporarily stop trading in a stock. Perhaps there is pending news or the exchange wants the company to disseminate a press release. The purpose is to allow investors enough time to absorb important information.

A trading suspension is the right of the SEC to stop trading for up to 10 days. It is a severe power that the SEC has and uses only sparingly. Typically, the SEC is concerned about possible manipulation or wrongdoing at a company and wants to investigate.

For a short seller, a trading suspension is the beginning of more bad news to come.

The SEC publishes its trading suspensions at: *http://www.sec. gov/litigation/suspensions.shtml*

TRIGGER EVENT 4:
UNEXPECTED LOSS/RESTATEMENT
OF EARNINGS

If a company reports an unexpected loss—that is, a loss that analysts did not forecast—a company will likely try to downplay the news and consider it a "one time" event. Short sellers, on the other hand, are not so easily convinced. It is often that an unexpected loss becomes expected for the next few quarters.

First, a company will likely guide analysts to a certain forecast number—making a surprise unlikely. Furthermore, a company often has discretion in finding reserves to make up for a shortfall.

So if a company cannot do the above, there might be a problem with the underlying business that is far from temporary.

Short sellers also are alerted when a company announces an earnings restatement. This can be the result of many things. But in most cases, it is because the company used aggressive accounting. Investors then begin to wonder if management has other things it is hiding.

TRIGGER EVENT 5: DELAYED FILINGS

A company must report its quarterly report within 45 days of the end of the quarter and its annual report no later than 90 days after the fiscal year. Investors and analysts (and short sellers) use this information on which to base their trading.

But what if the filings are not released on time? Short sellers might consider taking a short position.

If a company cannot file on time, it means that there is definitely a problem with the company. It could be that the company has an antiquated accounting and computer system. Or it could mean that the company is having a dispute with its auditor.

TRIGGER EVENT 6: REVERSE SPLITS

The most common stock split is when a company issues more shares to the shareholder base. Example: Suppose XYZ is selling for $100 per share. With such a high stock price, it might be difficult to attract investors. The company decides to do a 2-for-1 stock split. That is, each shareholder will get two shares for each owned. This means the number of shares on the market has doubled. Then again, there has been no change in the fundamentals of the company. So the stock price will fall by half to $50 per share.

As the name implies, a reverse split is the opposite of a split. Example: Let's say XYZ has had many problems and the stock price is at $1 per share. It can reduce the number of shares by taking away shares from the shareholder base. This will increase the stock price. If there is a 1-for-5 reverse split, a shareholder will have to turn in 5 shares for each owned. After the reverse split, the stock price will be $5.

True, in itself, a split or reverse split has no fundamental significance. But, it might have a signaling effect. This is an academic concept that goes as follows: A company believes its stock price will continue to increase, so it will split the stock. Or the company expects more problems—and the stock price to fall even more—so it decides to do a reverse split.

A professor at Houston State University conducted a study on reverse splits. For those splits between 1970 and 1992, he found that the stock prices, within three years, were down on average by a third.

TRIGGER EVENT 7:
DIVIDEND CUTS

The board of directors decides on whether to pay a dividend to shareholders. If the board decides to cut or cancel a dividend, this is a very positive sign for short sellers. It's a hint that the company is having difficulties with its cash flows and wants to preserve its capital as much as possible.

Short sellers might anticipate a dividend cut by using the following technique: comparing total dividends to the annual earnings per share (EPS). If the dividends are 80 percent or more of the EPS, a company might be tempted to cut or cancel the dividend.

TRIGGER EVENT 8:
REGULATORY ACTIONS

Compared to the rest of the world, the United States has a fairly open financial system. Even with the reforms of 2001, companies have lots of freedom to pursue their ventures.

However, companies can be overzealous and push the envelope. During 2002, we saw many examples of companies that used fraudulent accounting methods to artificially boost products. No doubt, short sellers are attuned to the government's responses to these.

But there are many other types of regulatory actions. Some of them might seem uneventful yet have a major impact on a company.

One type of regulatory action that interests short sellers is aggressive marketing. The FCC does not want companies to hype their products or make unfounded claims. If a company does so, the FCC can impose fines, as well as cease-and-desist orders. In fact, the company will likely be under intense scrutiny going forward.

What does this mean? The sales of the company could slow down because it is unable to continue its aggressive practices.

FIGHTING SHORT SELLERS

In some cases, a company will attack short sellers. These attacks come in a variety of forms, such as:

- *Threatening a lawsuit or filing one*: The reason is that the company believes that the short sellers are spreading false rumors. But, in many cases, these lawsuits are either settled or dropped.

- *Stock split or dividend*: A company might announce one of these. However, in order to be eligible for stock splits or dividends, shareholders need to send in their certificates to the company. For a short seller, this causes a big problem; that is, as shareholders take their shares out of street name, this is likely to result in a buy-in. Street name is when you keep your certificates with your broker. This is a much more convenient way to handle your stock holdings.

- *Request on street name*: A company might write a letter to shareholders asking them to take their shares out of street name. If this happens, it could result in a buy-in, which is discussed in the previous chapter.

Interestingly enough, if a company engages in these types of actions, it could be a good short sale opportunity. According to a study by Owen Lamont, a professor at the University of Chicago, he found that such attacks, on average, mean a –2-percent reduction in value for each month after.

Why? There are several possible reasons:

- The attacks might force short sellers to panic or might result in a buy-in. There is a short squeeze and the price surges to overvalued levels.
- The company does have real problems and is trying to externalize the blame on short sellers. Eventually, the real problems emerge and the stock price declines.

CONCLUSION

In this chapter, we set forth a framework that is based on discussions with a variety of short sellers. This framework should be very helpful in your analysis. But, of course, no framework is foolproof. Investing is not about absolute rules; it requires a certain amount of luck and intuition. This is the case even for the most sophisticated investors, such as Warren Buffett.

INTERPRETING FINANCIAL STATEMENTS

Many short sellers focus heavily on the financial statements of the company. On rare occasions, there might be obvious problems with the financials (for example, the numbers might not add up). But, for the most part, it takes a lot of digging to find red flags in financial statements. As the red flags accumulate, short sellers will start to build their case. This means lots of work—such as poring over the financials going back five years or so.

It is a painstaking process—but it is not beyond the individual investor. However, in order to do this, you need a strong foundation in financial statement analysis.

SOME HISTORY

Accounting has been in existence for thousands of years. Without it, companies would not be able to function. A company needs to be able to track its progress; investors need a way to gauge a business opportunity; and, of course, a government needs a way to tax companies.

It was during the 1400s that the fundamentals of modern accounting were established. Since then, there have been many modifications. As for the United States, there are a variety of sources of accounting rules that make up a body of standards known as GAAP, or generally accepted accounting principles. GAAP is the result of the rulings of organizations like the Securities and Exchange Commission, FASB (Financial Accounting Standards Board), and PCAOB (Public Company and Accounting Oversight Board). All public companies must abide by GAAP standards.

THE BIG THREE

Accounting involves the Big Three statements: balance sheet, income statement, and cash flow statement.

Let's first look at the balance sheet. It covers three things: a company's assets, liabilities, and equity. The formula is:

$$Assets = Liabilities + Capital$$

This formula is always correct because a company uses double-book entry accounting. That is, every transaction has two entries that are equal. Example: If a company buys equipment for $10,000, the Equipment category on the balance sheet will increase by $10,000 and the Cash category will fall by $10,000, keeping everything in balance.

Here's what a balance sheet looks like:

ASSETS	AMOUNTS
Current Assets	
Cash	10,000
Accounts Receivables	30,000
Inventories	20,000
Prepaid expenses	5,000
Total current assets	65,000
Noncurrent assets	
Land	100,000
Plant & Equipment	80,000
Accumulated Depreciation	20,000
Total Noncurrent Assets	160,000
Total Assets	225,000

LIABILITIES & EQUITY	AMOUNTS
Current Liabilities	
Accounts Payable	20,000
Notes Payable	30,000
Total Current Liabilities	50,000
Noncurrent Liabilities	
Long-Term Debt	50,000
Total Liabilities	100,000
Equity	
Common Stock	90,000
Retained Earnings	35,000
Total Equity	125,000
Total Liabilities and Equity	225,000

As you can see from above, the total assets of $225,000 equal the liabilities of $100,000 plus the equity of $125,000.

In terms of the assets, these are listed on the left side of the balance sheet in rank of liquidity. Current assets can typically be liquidated within a year or less. Noncurrent assets last more than a year.

The same goes for liabilities. Current liabilities are payable within a year, and noncurrent liabilities last longer.

There can be other asset, liability, and equity categories, but these are the main ones you will see. Here's the definition of each:

Cash: Cash balances, CDs, money markets and any other cash-type asset.

Accounts Receivables: What a customer owes the company for the sale of goods or the rendering of services.

Inventories: The raw materials and finished products that have yet to be sold to customers.

Prepaid Expenses: Prepayment for services that have yet to be rendered, such as rent or insurance.

Land: Any real property.

Plant & Equipment (P&E): Facilities and capital equipment. Over time, the P&E will lose value from wear-and-tear and obsolescence. This is accounted for in depreciation of the asset. These depreciation expenses are accumulated and subtracted for the original value of the P&E.

Accounts Payable: Amounts owed to suppliers and other vendors. These are typically payable within 30 days.

Notes Payable: Similar to accounts payable but the money is payable within a year.

Long-Term Debt: Amounts owed to a creditor that must be paid back after more than a year. These debts might also be in the form of bonds, which are notes sold to the general public and traded on exchanges.

Common Stock: The amount raised from outside investors.

Retained Earnings: Profits of the company that have not been distributed to shareholders in dividends.

BASIC ACCOUNTING PRINCIPLES

What makes good accounting is consistency. If the rules constantly change, it makes it difficult to provide analysis. To this end, there are bedrock accounting principles that underlie all financial statements:

Historical Cost: All categories on the financial statements are recorded at the original cost. Example: XYZ buys land for $100,000 and it is recorded on the balance sheet for this amount. Suppose that after 20 years, the value of the land is now worth $1 million.

According to the historical cost principle, the land is still valued at $100,000.

A smart investor will realize this and try to determine the market values of the assets on the balance sheet. A short seller, for example, might realize that a company's product line is obsolete and that its inventory is really not worth what it is expressed on the balance sheet. In other words, the value of the company is probably exaggerated.

Matching Principle: The revenues earned must be matched with the appropriate expenses incurred. It might be tempting for a company to recognize the revenues sooner and delay the expenses, which boosts overall profitability.

Periodicity: As stated at the start of this chapter, investors look at trends. This is why financial statements are generated on a periodic basis, usually quarterly.

THE INCOME STATEMENT

The income statement shows whether or not a company is profitable. Of all the statements, it is this one that is subject to the most manipulation and where short sellers find crucial red flags.

Here's a sample income statement:

Net Sales	10,000
Cost of Goods Sold	4,000
Gross Profits	6,000
Operating Expenses	
Selling, General, and Administration	3,000
Depreciation and Amortization	1,000
Income from Operations	2,000
Other Income and Expenses	
Interest Expense	500
Dividend and Interest Income	100
Income Before Income Taxes	1,600
Taxes	400
Net Income	1,200
Earnings Per Share	$1.20

Let's take a step-by-step look at how this statement works:

Net Sales: These are the proceeds from the sales of goods or services. If there are rebates or discounts, these are adjusted and the result is Net Sales.

Cost of Goods Sold: These are the costs that are directly related to the Net Sales of the product. Such costs would include inventory, labor, and shipping.

Gross Profits: The gain on sales that exclude operating expenses. A key ratio is the gross profit margin, which is:

Gross Profits/Net Sales

If this deteriorates over time, a short seller is alerted. The company could be experiencing deterioration of its core business.

Operating Profits: These are the costs that are necessary to run the business regardless if there are any sales or not. Included is also depreciation and amortization. These are called noncash expenses because there are no out-of-pocket expenses for the company.

Net Income: The profit a company generates after all expenses have been incurred.

Earnings per Share: This is the following:

Net Income/Number of shares outstanding

In our example, we assume that there are 1200 shares outstanding, so the EPS (earnings per share is):

$$\$1.20 = \$1200/1200$$

CASH FLOW STATEMENT

Some investors confuse profits with cash flow. They are not the same. Profit is an accounting concept based on a variety of principles. A company can show a profit and yet have negative cash flow. How is this possible? As seen above, a company can accelerate revenues or defer the recognition of expenses. There are also noncash expenses, such as depreciation.

The cash flow statement combines these effects and shows how much money a company is bringing in or flowing out.

Here's a sample cash flow statement, which consists of three sections:

Cash Flows from Operating Activities: This section shows those cash flows from the ongoing business activity with customers.

Net Income	5,000
Adjustments to Net Income	
Depreciation	+1,000
Increase in Accounts Receivables	−500
Increase in Accounts Payables	+200
Net Cash Provided by Operating Activities	5,700

First, the net income is taken from the company's income statement. The depreciation is added to the net income because this is a noncash expense.

Any increase in current assets requires an expenditure from the company. A decrease means an inflow.

In our example, the increase in accounts receivables means that the company did not receive any cash for its sale. Furthermore, if there had been an increase in inventory, this would have meant more expenditures for the company and thus reduced operating cash flows.

On the other hand, an increase in current liabilities will boost cash flow and vice versa. By increasing its accounts payable, the company did not have to pay for its assets (at least not for now). But if the liability fell, then it had to use cash to pay for it.

Cash Flows from Investing Activities: A company might make large investments in plant and equipment, stocks, bonds, or other companies.

Payments for Property, Plant & Equipment	3,000
Proceeds from the Sale of a Company	2,000

The first line is known as capital expenditures, or cap-ex for short. Such investments reduce the cash flow of the company.

Then again, a company might decide to sell off capital assets, such as a (company or subsidiary). This increases the cash flow of the company.

Cash Flows from Financing Activities: The company can engage in a variety of financing activities, such as issuing stocks or bonds.

Proceeds from the issuance of bonds	2,000
Payment of long-term debt	1,000
Purchase of company stock	3,000
Dividends paid	100
Proceeds from the issuance of common stock	500

Cash flow is increased if a company raises money from:

* Debt offering
* Equity offering

Cash flows are reduced if a company:

* Pays dividends
* Pays off debt
* Repurchases it stock on the open market

FREE CASH FLOW

The cash flow statement is not perfect. After all, which category should you look at? Many short sellers will recast the cash flow statement to determine a company's free cash flow. Essentially, the free cash flow is any money left over after all necessary expenditures are made.

There is no single way to calculate free cash flow. But here is one approach that is fairly straightforward:

Step 1: Use the Operating Cash Flows from Operating Activities (OCFOA)

Step 2: Reduce the OCFOA by the tax deduction received from the exercise of employee stock options

Step 3: Add the cap-ex numbers from the Statement of Investing Activities and reduce these from the figure in Step 2.

Step 4: If there were any one-time amounts on the OCFOA, then eliminate them.

THE FILINGS

By law, a company is required to make quarterly and annual filings of their income statement, balance sheet, and cash flow statement. You can typically find these from:

* Financial sites (*quote.yahoo.com*, *multex.com*)
* The company's Web site

- The company's Investor Relations Department (call them and they should send you paper filings)

From the main filings you will locate the Big Three:

10-Q: The quarterly statement, which is for the first, second, and third quarters for a company.

10-K: This is the annual document, which also includes the results for the fourth quarter.

Annual Report: This is not as comprehensive as the 10-K. In fact, it is usually a glossy document but can still be very useful.

CONCLUSION

At first, the Big Three statements can seem somewhat daunting. But over time, they will start to become second nature. All short sellers need to go through this process (in fact, any investor should).

In this next chapter, we look at ways the short sellers use financial statements to identify short sale candidates.

THE RED FLAG CHECKLIST

If you are new to accounting, it is probably worth rereading the prior chapter. It can be somewhat overwhelming at first. But it is essential; all good short sellers have a strong grasp of the working of the Big Three statements.

With a foundation in financial statement analysis, you can then start to detect the red flags. In this chapter, we look at each statement and provide a checklist of the types of red flags a short seller would be interested in.

BALANCE SHEET

A short seller will often say that a company has a "deteriorating balance sheet." The big red flags revolve around increased debt and artificially inflated assets.

Here's the checklist:

BURN RATE VERSUS CASH IN THE BANK

If a company is losing money, how long will it take for it to run out? This is known as looking at the burn rate. To estimate the burn rate, you can do the following:

Step 1: Take the average negative operating cash flows for the past two quarters.

Step 2: Take the result from Step 1 and multiply it by 2. This is known as annualizing the cash flow (assuming the cash flow is the same for each quarter).

Step 3: Divide the Cash on the balance sheet from Step 2.

This is a very rough measure. After all, a company might be able to raise more money by issuing more stock or debt. Or the company might turn around and improve on its cash flows.

However, if things remain the same and the company has less than a year left to fund its operations, the risk level is certainly high.

DETERIORATION IN ALLOWANCE FOR DOUBTFUL ACCOUNTS

When a company sells a product and gets a promise of future payment, there is a new asset called accounts receivable. If the customer does not pay the amount, the company needs to write off this asset and reduce its sales.

In GAAP accounting, a company is required to estimate the probability of customers not paying their bills. What should the amount be? There is much discretion on the part of the company, and thus it is tempting to underestimate it. In other words, this artificially inflates sales.

Short sellers see a red flag if:

- The allowance for doubtful accounts is not increasing even though the industry is slumping.
- The allowance for doubtful accounts is significantly lower than industry peers.

INCREASES IN SOFT ACCOUNTS

To capitalize an expense means to essentially convert an expense into an asset. This tends to increase profits because the expenses are lower.

Suppose a company spends $10 million on advertising. If the company believes that $5 million of the expenses will benefit the firm for several years, then the full $10 million should not be expensed. Instead, $5 million should be capitalized into an asset and then reduced over the next few years.

Short sellers often find capitalized expenses in the prepaid expenses category on the balance sheet. Or these expenses could be hidden in soft accounts, such as "other current assets" or "other noncurrent assets."

Growth in these types of assets would be an alert for a short seller.

BEWARE OF TOXIC EQUITY

Suppose XYZ is experiencing major problems. But, in the most recent announcement, the company was able to raise $40 million by issuing shares. On the face of it, this sounds great.

There is no question that capital is a good thing for a company. But this can be deceiving.

A savvy short seller will look at the following:

First question: Is the company getting money because it is cheap and the stock is overpriced?

A company can issue more stock to the public—which is called a secondary offering. This often happens when management believes that the stock price is at an unsustainable price. Might as well raise money while you can, right?

Also, look at where the money is going. If a large percentage is going to senior officers and major shareholders, then the company will not have this money available to it.

The second question: What price did the offering exact for the company? In a secondary offering, the terms are very favorable. The stock price is typically high and, as a result, existing shareholders do not suffer much dilution. On the other hand, a company might be in dire straights and desperate for money. A company might agree to just about anything to get more capital.

Generally, these financings are known as PIPEs (private investments in public entities). In a PIPE financing, a company does not sell shares to the general public; instead, the buyers are institutions and wealthy individuals. This is known as a private placement. Because the investors are considered to be sophisticated, the disclosure and filing requirements are not as stringent as a secondary offering.

But the terms are often tough for the firm. Short sellers will be alerted if they see such things as:

- The investors get shares at a discount to the current stock price.
- The investors have a conversion right. If a stock price falls below certain price thresholds, investors will get more and more shares. This can have a highly dilutive effect on a company.
- The investors get liquidation rights. Thus, if the company goes into bankruptcy, the investors get any proceeds before all other shareholders do.

Because of the above factors, short sellers find many prospective candidates from companies that engage in PIPE financings.

Note: Analyzing debt is a crucial part of a short seller's job. We cover this in depth in Chapter 8.

INCOME STATEMENT

There are a variety of key red flags that a short seller looks for when analyzing the income statement:

DETERIORATION IN SALES

The sales of a company can be volatile. There might be a new product introduction or a recession. The sales might be seasonal (for example, a large portion of a retailer's sales come from the fourth quarter).

The short seller is looking for adverse trends in sales that result from such factors as heavy competition, quality problems, or market saturation.

Here are some tips:

- Pricing: Some companies have strong pricing power. This might be the result of legal protection (like a patent) or a strong brand (an example would be Starbucks). However, many companies do not have pricing power. In fact, when prices start to fall, it is usually only the start of a worsening trend. So look for weaknesses in pricing of a company's major products.

- Saturation: All industries go through life cycles. In the early stages, the growth rates can be hefty. At some point, the market is saturated and it becomes much more difficult for companies to grow. Short sellers try to find these inflection points. Basically, a short seller will look at overall industry penetration rates. If they are 80 percent or more, saturation is near.

- Acquisitions: This can be a method for a company to keep pumping up sales, especially if the industry is reaching saturation. This can work for several years. But M&A is a tricky business and difficult to manage. At some point, a company's growth rate will slow down.

- Segmented Sales: A company might have different product or service divisions. But, in most cases, one division will represent the lion's share of sales. If a company's core business is faltering, it is tempting for management to focus attention on other divisions. These divisions might help mask the deterioration.

Finally, technology companies are prone to big surges in sales and then flameout. The main reason is that a technology company will usually have one flagship product. But as competition sets in, prices fall, and the market can be easily saturated.

CASH FLOW STATEMENT

As we saw in the last chapter, the cash flow statement is often the most accurate reflection of a company's overall health. This is why short sellers pay lots of attention to this part of a company's financials. Short sellers look for reality.

Also, savvy short sellers will look at a company's free cash flow (which we defined in the last chapter).

Here's a short seller's checklist for the cash flow statement:

FREE CASH FLOW VERSUS NET INCOME

Short sellers look for those companies that show growing net income, yet free cash flow is declining or even negative. The implication is that management is attempting to artificially inflate net income.

A classic example of this was the high-flier telecom company Lucent. From 1998 to 1999, the company was posting strong gains in its earnings on the income statement. But after calculating the free cash flow, the company was actually hemorrhaging.

The key reasons included high capital expenditures and a deteriorating balance sheet (in other words, too much growth in accounts receivables and inventories).

A short seller might use an obscure ratio called the quality of earning ratio. The formula is:

Step 1: Net income − Free cash flow = Net income differential

Step 2: (Average total assets for quarter X + Average total assets for quarter Y)/2 = Average total assets

Step 3: Net income differential/average total assets = Quality of earnings ratio

If you see a ratio of 0.03 or more, it is a sign of quality problems with the company's earnings.

LOOK FOR ERRATIC CASH FLOWS

If you look at annual financial statements, it might look like a company has strong cash flows. Then again, if you analyze the quarter-by-quarter changes, it might be quite erratic. A short seller might take this as a sign of manipulation.

This is what happened with Enron. Here's how erratic its cash flows were:

Q2 2000	–$90 million
Q3 2000	$674 million
Q4 2000	$4.6 billion

Q1 2001   –$464 million
Q2 2001   –$873 million

CONCLUSION

Certainly, there are a variety of other red flags that short sellers can spot from a company's financial statements. However, the red flags covered in this chapter are fairly representative of what short sellers have in their arsenal of tools. As you spend more time on the financials, you will spot your own trends and perhaps come up with your own techniques.

In the next chapter, we look at using ratio analysis for financial statements.

CHAPTER 8

RATIO ANALYSIS

A fruitful tool for short sellers is ratio analysis. For those who have math phobia, you have nothing to fear. Ratios are fairly simple. Interestingly enough, you should not have to actually calculate them yourself because most top Web sites have already done this for you, such as *Multex.com* and *Yahoo.com*.

Mathematically, a ratio is just a comparison. Short sellers can use ratios to help makes sense of the balance sheet, income statement, and cash flow statements.

RATIO BASICS

Suppose a company has a price earnings ratio (P/E ratio) of 55. What does this mean? Should you short it? Not necessarily. Ratios have very little meaning if they are not put into a proper context. In our example, suppose that the company is in an industry where the average PE is 25. If there is no good explanation for justifying the premium valuation over its peers, the company's stock might indeed be overvalued and a potentially good short sale candidate.

Generally, short sellers like to make industry comparisons with financial ratios. Short sellers also like to see the trends in the ratios. Have they been deteriorating over the past few years? Are a company's ratios worse than the industry average?

CURRENT RATIO/QUICK RATIO

The ultimate goal for short sellers is to see a company go bust and its stock price plunge to zero. This means gauging the liquidity of the company; that is, does the company have enough resources to the pay the bills?

There are a variety of liquidity-type ratios. In fact, many lenders will require a company to maintain minimum levels of these ratios when providing debt financing.

One helpful ratio is the current ratio, which is:

$$\text{Current Assets/Current Liabilities}$$

If this is less than 1.0, then a company could have liquidity problems. However, this ratio has some limitations. For instance, the current assets might be inflated. The usual culprit is the inventory, which can be difficult to sell off.

Short sellers, as a result, might focus on the quick ratio, which excludes inventory:

$$\text{(Current Assets—Inventory)/Current Liabilities}$$

In some cases, a short seller might get ultraconservative and refine the equation to include only the most liquid assets:

$$\text{(Cash and Marketable Securities)/Current Liabilities}$$

INVENTORY/ACCOUNTS RECEIVABLE RATIOS

In the last chapter, we learned that short sellers pay close attention to trends in inventories and accounts receivables. There are also some good ratios to help with the analysis:

Inventory Turnover Ratio: The formulas is:

$$(\text{Inventory for Time period 1} + \text{Inventory for Time Period 2})/2$$
$$= \text{Average Inventory}$$

COST OF GOODS SOLD (COGS)/ AVERAGE INVENTORY

The COGS shows the value of the inventory that has been sold and the average inventory value in the warehouses. Suppose XYZ has $10 million in COGS and $5 million in average inventory for the past quarter. This means XYZ turns over its inventory twice every quarter.

A short seller will want to see the turnover deteriorate over time. This indicates that a company is having problems selling its goods.

Accounts Receivables Turnover: The formula is:

$$(\text{Accounts Receivables for Period 1} +$$
$$\text{Accounts Receivables for Period 2})/2$$

SALES/AVERAGE ACCOUNTS RECEIVABLES

This parallels the concept of the inventory turnover ratio. With the accounts receivable turnover ratio, you get an idea of how long it takes to convert credit sales into cash. A short seller wants to see this lengthen.

PRICE-EARNINGS RATIO

The price-earnings (PE) ratio is fairly controversial. Some short sellers believe that it does not impart much information. But there are enough short sellers who give it credence—so, it is something to definitely consider.

The PE ratio helps investors compare valuations among companies. The formula is:

$$\text{PE} = \text{Stock Price}/\text{Earnings Per Share (EPS)}$$

EPS is usually for the past 12 months. But some short sellers will actually compute a forward-looking PE ratio, which uses an EPS forecast for the next 12 months. This approach is a little more dicey because estimates can prove to be wrong.

Short sellers, though, might use this to their advantage. Suppose the PE ratio is still high even if a company meets the most optimistic estimates. In this case, a company's stock could plunge if it fails to meet its targets.

The PE ratio could be a useless figure if a company does not have any earnings. Or the earnings might be greatly depressed because of a recession.

PEG RATIO

Let's say a company has a PE ratio of 300. Many investors would consider this a steep price to pay for the stock. Some short sellers might also be tempted to make a short sale transaction.

Be careful. Markets will give a company a high PE ratio if the firm can grow at a rapid pace. This is what happened with eBay. While the PE was high, the fact remained that the company was growing its earnings at a super-fast rate.

Thus an investor must look at a PE ratio in terms of a company's growth in earnings. This can be done with the PEG ratio:

P-E Ratio / Growth Rate

What metrics should you use? The Motley Fool has developed its own system:

0.50 or less	Buy
0.50 to 0.65	Look to buy
0.65 to 1.00	Hold
1.00 to 1.30	Look to sell
1.30 to 1.70	Consider shorting
Over 1.70	Short

Keep in mind that this system is not foolproof (no system really is). Some short sellers, for example, might want for the PEG ratio to go over 1.70. Or a short seller might begin to take a short position at 1.50 or so, although, the 1.70 level has been fairly successful for the short positions of the Fool.

PRICE-TO-SALES RATIO

As seen above, if a company has no earnings, a PE ratio is meaningless. An alternative in this situation is to use the Price-to-Sales Ratio (PSR):

Market Capitalization/Sales for the past 12 months

The market capitalization is the value of a company according to Wall Street. The formula is:

Stock Price × Shares Outstanding

Suppose XYZ has 50 million shares on the market and the stock price is $10. The market cap would be $500 million. If the sales are $100 million, then the PSR is 5.0.

Ken Fisher, who is a money manager and newsletter publisher, has done extensive study on the PSR. He also wrote about his findings in his classic book, *Super Stocks*. According to him, he thinks companies reach overvaluation when the PSR exceeds 3.0.

PRICE-TO-BOOK RATIO

The price-to-book ratio provides a guide to a company's relative valuation. The book value is as follows:

Assets − Liabilities

Generally, the higher the book value, the more wealth a company has. But this can be deceiving. The value of a company's assets could depreciate: The inventory might be unsellable, plant and equipment might become obsolete, or the accounts receivable might be uncollectible.

Market Cap and Enterprise Value

Short sellers like keeping track of a company's market cap. Sometimes, the level can reach ridiculous proportions. For instance, during the dot-com craze, the market cap of *Priceline.com* was bigger than all the market caps of the airlines in the United States. How could that be justified? It couldn't. And short sellers realized this.

Short sellers also like to use a more refined version of market cap: the enterprise value. The formula is as follows:

Enterprise value = Market Cap + Debt – Cash

The reason debt is added to market cap is that, in the event of a takeover, the buyer would assume the debt. This is a cost to the buyer; that is, the debt increases the value of the company. On the other hand, the buyer can use the cash to pay down its debt, which lowers the valuation of the firm.

If a company has a very high market cap and debt, but little cash, the valuation could be quite steep—giving more ammunition to short sellers.

Despite this, the price-to-book ratio can still be a good approximation. The formula for the ratio is:

Stock Price/Book Value Per Share

In fact, this valuation metric is a bit more stable because book value typically does not change much—this is in contrast to a company's earnings, which can be quite volatile.

A caveat: Some industries do not have high book values. Instead, the value might be in the form of intellectual property or other intangible assets. Traditionally, these types of assets are greatly undervalued on a company's balance sheet. So a company like Microsoft could have a high price-to-book ratio, but still not necessarily be overvalued.

Short sellers like to find company's with book values below 1. This is an indication of serious problems with a company. For instance, this was the case with Smith Corona, a leading typewriter company. No doubt, if you looked at the company's balance sheet, it was rich in assets. But the company's core business was rapidly being eroded by competing technologies.

RETURN ON EQUITY/RETURN ON ASSETS

The return on equity is calculated as:

$$\text{Net Profits/Shareholder's Equity}$$

Return on equity is a key ratio for investors. How much return is a company's management providing in relation to invested capital? Short sellers are encouraged if this is declining, but, they might also be heartened if it is growing.

The reason is that the return on equity (ROE) ratio can be deceptive. Let's take two companies as an example:

COMPANY	NET INCOME	ASSETS	LIABILITIES	ROE
ABC	$5 million	$100 million	$50 million	10%
XYZ	$5 million	$100 million	$0	5%

Just looking at the ROE, ABC appears to be stronger. However, the reason for this is simple: ABC has borrowed much more money, which reduces the equity portion of the ratio. In other words, a company can pump up the ROE by leveraging its balance sheet.

This is not necessarily a bad thing, but it does increase the overall risk of the company. Furthermore, look at other companies in the industry. Some industries should have lower amounts of debt because of the volatility. But if a company is piling on a lot of debt, it could be an ominous sign of problems.

To wash out the effects of debt, you can compute the return on assets (ROA) ratio:

$$\text{Net Income/Total Assets}$$

In our example, both ABC and XYZ would have the same ratio: 5 percent. Short sellers like to see companies with relatively high valuation yet a small ROA ratio. These are typically slow-growth companies, but the market might not realize it yet. For example, this appears to be what happened with McDonald's. It is a company rich in assets—but a slowing growth rate. For example, it's ROA was less than 4 percent, which is not the sign of a growth company (a better ratio would have been 10 percent). So it should not be surprising that the company's stock price begun a steep fall, going from the $50 dollar range in early 2002 to about $12 three years later.

DEBT-TO-EQUITY RATIO

The debt-to-equity ratio is:

Long-term Debt/Shareholder's Equity

This is a crucial element in getting a sense if a company could be in jeopardy of liquidity problems or even bankruptcy. Short sellers look for a rapid rise in this ratio—along with overall deterioration of the business.

A short seller might also factor in off-balance-sheet liabilities. These are liabilities that are disclosed in the footnotes of a company's financial statements but do not appear on the balance sheet.

These off-balance-sheet assets typically include:

Operating Lease: A lease allows a company the use of property for a fixed period in return for periodic rent payments. A capital lease allows the company to retain ownership of the property when the lease expires. An operating lease does not, and according to accounting rules, is not required to be reported on a company's balance sheet. But if the lease is long term (say more than 10 years), a short seller will likely consider it to be a liability.

Special Purpose Entities (SPE): This is similar to a joint venture that typically engages in risky activity—which a company does not want to affect its balance sheet. These are extremely complex vehicles, but they are listed in the footnotes of the financials. In fact, Enron commonly used SPEs to hide its growing debt.

Pension Liabilities: Some companies offer their employees defined benefit plans. As the name implies, a company is obligated to pay a fixed amount to its employees when they retire. To pay for these obligations, a company will set aside funds in a trust that will hopefully grow over time. But what if the liabilities grow, but not the trust? The pension will be underfunded, which represents a liability. Some of these liabilities can be quite substantial.

To calculate the debt-to-equity ratio that includes off-balance-sheet liabilities, you would do the following:

$$(\text{Long-term debt} + \text{Off-balance-sheet debt})/ \text{Shareholder's equity}$$

TIMES INTEREST EARNED

The times earnest earned ratio (which is also referred to as the coverage ratio) is:

$$\text{Income before interest and taxes}/\text{Interest expense}$$

Banks like to use this ratio when structuring financials. A typical ratio would be for a company to maintain 4.0 or better. In many cases, you can find the loan agreements by downloading a company's SEC documents from EDGAR. If a short seller notices that the ratio is getting close to the minimum, it could mean problems.

CONCLUSION

It is important to emphasize the idea that short sellers use ratios in context of the industry. How does the inventory turnover compare to a company's peers? Also, short sellers spend a lot of time focusing on the trends in the ratios. Are the trends worsening?

DISCOUNTED CASH FLOW ANALYSIS

Ratio analysis is fairly easy in terms of math. But this does not detract from its analytical powers.

Of course, there are more complex modelings a short seller can engage in. These require sophisticated spreadsheets and advanced equations. Most definitely, this requires a graduate-level background in finance.

But don't despair. Top online financial sites do provide some sophisticated modeling.

One of the most common is the discounted cash flow (DCF) method. This is what many top Wall Street analysts use. It is also a preferred method in academia.

The premise is that the value of a stock is the present value of a company's future cash flows. The higher the cash flows, the higher the stock. The problem is: How do you calculate the cash flows? This requires a lot of analytical work. Also, because these are projections, the DCF method must account for risk of a firm not producing the cash flows. This is done using a discount rate. The more uncertain a firm, the higher the discount rate.

You can use the power of DCF at the Quicken Web site (*www.quicken.com*), which they call the Intrinsic Value Calculator.

To see it work, let's use McDonald's as an example. First, you enter the company's ticker, MCD. Next, you input the projected growth rate in earnings. You can use different methods (analyst's projections, the average growth rate for the past five years and so on). I used the growth rate for the past five years of 7.45 percent. Finally, you enter the discount rate. Quicken suggested 15 percent, which is what I used.

The results? According to Quicken, the intrinsic value of the stock was $4.84 and the current stock price was $14.84. Using this method, it would seem like a good short sale candidate.

Thankfully, there are enough online resources that calculate the ratios for you. Of course, the key is that you need to understand how to interpret them—which is often a process that is both a science and an art.

In the next chapter, we look at bankruptcy.

CHAPTER 9

THE JOYS OF BANKRUPTCY

The dream of all short sellers is to find a stock that plunges to zero. Generally, a stock falls to zero because of one reason: bankruptcy.

True, bankruptcy occurs mainly during bear markets and recessions. But there are certainly examples when companies have gone bust during booms.

How can you spot potential bankruptcy situations? Like everything else in investing, the process is more art than science. Yet there are some factors to consider.

WHAT IS BANKRUPTCY?

A company has three sources of financing:

Equity: Investors buy ownership in the company and get shares.
Debt: Individuals, companies, and institutions lend cash to the company.
Cash Flow: A company generates cash from selling its products and services for a profit.

A company falls into bankruptcy when it is unable to pay its outstanding debts to its creditors. This sounds simple, yet it is an extremely complex process. There is extensive federal legislation that governs corporate bankruptcies. The process is handled by a federal judge and can easily take several years.

The goal of bankruptcy is not to punish a company; rather, it is meant to allow for a fresh start. There are a variety of examples of companies that have sunk into bankruptcy and reemerged as successful enterprises.

The downside is: shareholders. In order to allow the company to survive, the shareholders are usually wiped out. According to the bankruptcy law, the shareholders are last in line to receive any of the proceeds from a liquidation. The creditors get first dibs.

There are two types of corporate bankruptcy filings:

- *Chapter 11*: This is known as a reorganization. When filed, all lawsuits are stopped and a company can get quick and easy financing to stay afloat. A federal judge will oversee the process, and the bankrupt company will submit a reorganization plan to turn around the situation.
- *Chapter 7*: There is little hope of the company returning to health. So the assets are liquidated and creditors are paid something (in most cases, just pennies on the dollar).

Whichever filing is selected, the results are usually the same: shareholders are wiped out.

In the rest of this chapter, we look at key signs that a company could be poised for bankruptcy.

UPCOMING DEBT PAYMENTS

Debt is a two-edged sword. It can be an effective method for growing a company. On the other hand, if problems arise, such as a fall in cash flows, a company could have difficulty paying the interest and principal on the debt. Bankruptcy might be inevitable.

A short seller will look at several things:

- What is the trend of the debt? If it is growing faster than sales and is higher than industry peers, the risk of bankruptcy increases.

- Are there any principal payments due in the near future? Suppose a company has cash in the bank of $10 million and cash flow of $1 million. Unfortunately, there is a debt payment of $20 million due in six months. This would be a huge problem for the company and could mean bankruptcy.

DRAWDOWN ON A CREDIT LINE

A credit line is financing that is readily available at any time. Companies typically use it for short-term squeezes. For example, during the fourth quarter, a retailer might need to use its credit line to handle inventory purchases.

Short sellers, though, are alerted when a company completely draws down its credit line. This is an indication that there is trouble. After all, the company is taking the money now just in case it is unavailable because it is unable to meet certain requirements of the credit line agreement because of deterioration of the business.

PRICE OF CORPORATE BONDS

On the balance sheet, you can find the bonds a company has issued to finance its activities. A short seller will look at the quotes of these bonds. You can, too, by looking at such sites as *bonds.yahoo.com*.

Most bonds are issued to investors at $1000 a piece—known as the face value. After that, investors will buy and sell bonds in the open market. The price will depend on a variety of factors, such as the level of interest rates. But if the company is experiencing problems, the bond price should fall. If the problems become dire, the bonds might sell at pennies on the dollar. Short sellers like to see this—especially if the stock price does not seem to reflect the skepticism.

A top analyst at Dresdner Kleinwort Wasserstein, Henry Miller, has guidelines for analyzing the prices of corporate bonds:

- 80 to 90 cents on the dollar: This raises some concern. This could be the first indication of problems.
- 60 cents to 80 cents: The concerns are justified. The chances of things getting worse are real.
- 40 to 60 cents: Bankruptcy is a major possibility.
- 40 cents or below: A filing is likely any time.

For Miller, a good short sale candidate is when the price range is between 40 to 60 cents.

THE FILING

Suppose a company files for bankruptcy. Is it too late to short the stock? Not necessarily. In some cases, there might be die-hard believers in the company. Or these investors might not really understand the bankruptcy process.

Companies such as Enron still provided short sellers with profit opportunities after bankruptcy filings. Keep in mind, however, that it could be difficult to borrow these shares.

RECESSION

Suppose you find a company that meets the criteria in this chapter. Moreover, the company has several other red flags, which we discussed in Chapter 5.

If the economy is growing, the chances of bankruptcy might not necessarily be significant. On the other hand, if the economy is in recession, bankruptcy could be a self-fulfilling prophesy. A recession is defined as two consecutive quarters of negative growth in a country's gross domestic product (GDP), which is the amount of goods and services produced in an economy. During a recession:

- Many companies show declines in revenues and profits.

- Customers and suppliers might be concerned and demand stronger terms.

- The credit markets are tight and it could be extremely difficult to borrow money.

- The stock price is very low, making it nearly impossible to raise money by selling shares.

With such factors, a company that is already on the edge could easily fall into bankruptcy.

THE MYSTERIOUS BUSINESS OF CREDIT ANALYSIS

There are different types of Wall Street analysts. There are those that analyze the common stock and look for growth opportunities. Then there are credit analysts that focus on the bonds and other debt of a company. Credit analysts are not necessarily concerned with the potential growth; rather, they want to determine the probability of default.

The most well-known credit analysts are S&P and Moody's. However, these organizations are not perfect. After all, they had strong credit ratings on companies like WorldCom and Enron—not long before the companies went bust.

But some of the smaller credit analysts had more accurate assessments. One of the firms was Fitch's. A senior analyst, Ralph Pellecchia, was bearish on Enron several years before the meltdown. Here's how he describes his analytical approach:

"The assessment process is itself a blend of quantitative and qualitative factors. Quantitative factors that are parts of the rating process include an evaluation of published financial information, supplemental financial information and peer financial performance. Qualitative factors include business fundamentals, competitive position, growth opportunities, the regulatory environment and our view as to the abilities of management."

From *http://www.senate.gov/~gov_affairs/032002pellecchia.htm.*

In a way, a credit analyst asks the same types of questions a short seller would.

FINANCIAL INSTITUTIONS AND CONFIDENCE

Financial firms have a special place in the economy. They allow for the smooth functioning of commerce. A crucial part of the success of a financial firm—such as a bank, insurance company, and brokerage—is trust. If customers lose confidence, they might stampede to withdraw their funds, and the firm collapses.

Such runs on financial firms have been a recurring theme. It happened on a wide scale in the 1930s, when the U.S. banking system virtually collapsed, and even during the late 1980s, when the savings and loans went bust.

Because of the possibility of a sudden plunge into bankruptcy, short sellers often focus on finance firms. One of the top short sellers, James Chanos, made significant returns shorting savings and loans during the late 1980s.

Some factors to look for in a financial firm that might be facing a loss of confidence include:

- A sudden and unexpected quarterly loss
- A write down of a large percentage of loans (say 10 percent of the portfolio)
- An investigation by the SEC or other federal regulators

CONCLUSION

Bankruptcy means that a company is unable to pay its *debts*. But what if a company does not have much debt? In this case, the chances of bankruptcy are slim. It is nearly impossible.

So short sellers like to focus on companies that have large amounts of debt. Of course, this is not the only indicator to consider. But it is a strong indicator, especially if a company is having trouble generating sufficient cash flows.

OTHER COMPANY FILINGS

Ashort seller will spend much time analyzing the financial statements included in a company's 10-Ks and 10-Qs. But there are other statements a short seller will look at, as well. These include:

- Proxies
- Form 4s—Insider Sales
- Annual Reports
- 8-Ks
- Press releases
- S-1s

Let's take a closer look at each.

PROXY STATEMENTS

Shareholders have a right to vote on important matters, such as directors, mergers, and so on. At least once a year, a company must have an annual meeting where votes are taken. To make informed decisions, a company is required to send each shareholder a proxy statement.

A proxy statement ranges from 40 to 100 pages. Short sellers will spend time perusing the document, focusing on matters like:

Executive Compensation: This can make for fun reading. You might see corporate jets, lucrative pensions, and country club memberships. There is nothing necessarily wrong with perks—they can be a great way to attract top talent.

Then again, a short seller will want to find signs of largesse:

- Is the compensation much higher than the industry standard?
- Are there "can't lose" compensation arrangements, such as guaranteed bonuses?
- Are there any lifetime perks (such as use of the corporate jet)?
- Is compensation increasing even though profits are falling?

Management Team: The proxy has the bios of the senior managers and directors. When reviewing these bios, does it look like the company has a weak team? Is there enough experience to carry the company forward?

Related-Party Transactions: This might be a case where a XYZ Corp. is doing business with ABC Corp. and an executive is an owner or director of ABC Corp. Or, suppose XYZ Corp. is doing business with a relative of an executive of XYZ Corp.

These transactions are not per se illegal, so long as they are disclosed. The problem is: Does the deal make sense? Was XYZ getting a good deal? Or was there favoritism?

Shareholder Proposals: Shareholders have the right to make proposals to be voted on for the proxy statement. A short seller likes companies that have several such proposals because it is indication of discontent. Pay attention to proposals regarding compensation, staggered boards, and accounting policies.

FORM 4S—INSIDER SALES

Executives not only get nice salaries, but they also have access to insider information. During the 1930s, Congress passed laws to protect investors and allow for a more level playing field. Congress could have easily forbade executives trading in their own shares, but this seemed too restrictive. Instead, it was okay for executives to buy or sell stock in their own company's shares so long as there was disclosure.

Perhaps because of the fact that communications was much slower in the 1930s, the deadlines for such disclosures could be up to as much as 40 days from the trade. With the scandals of 2002, Congress passed a new law, called the Sarbanes-Oxley Act, which shrunk the deadline to only two business days.

These disclosures are known as "insider trades." An insider is defined as a person that is an executive, director, or major shareholder (holding at least 10 percent of the company's stock).

Generally, when insiders buy shares, this is a very bullish sign. Why else would they buy except to make money?

Insider shares are a bit more ambiguous. An insider might sell because of a divorce or a tax bill or to diversify holdings. It might have little to do with the prospects of the company.

But this does not mean short sellers ignore insider sales. As we saw in Chapter 2, James Chanos noticed heavy insider selling at Enron before the company's stock price plunged.

Some of the signs short sellers look for in insider selling include:

- Cluster Selling: When several insiders sell large amounts of stock. A big amount would be 10 percent or more of an insider's total holdings.
- Selling on Rallies: If the stock has been falling, but you notice insider selling on minor rallies, this is a good sign for short sellers.
- Selling at new lows: If the stock is hitting 52-week lows and yet insiders are still selling, the stock is likely to fall further.

ANNUAL REPORTS

As the name implies, the annual report is management's disclosure to shareholders about the prior year. It is not as comprehensive as the 10-K, nor as complex. Generally, the annual report is a marketing document for shareholders—to try to keep them as shareholders or perhaps even get them to buy more shares.

An annual report can be quite glitzy, with nice pictures and lots of smiling faces (especially from senior management). Despite the fluff, short sellers can find nuggets of useful information.

Areas of focus for the short seller:

Chairman's Letter: This is often upbeat. Then again, if it has a negative tone—and it has been negative for several years—this could be a good short sale candidate.

You should also look for trigger words, such as "challenging" or "difficult" or "pressing." These are red flags that short sellers pick up on.

Promises: Look at the annual reports for the past five years. Did the Chairman make promises and not deliver? Was there a major initiative announced and then not mentioned it in subsequent years? These are signs of problems at the company.

Business Model: The Chairman should make a case for the company's business model and competitive advantage. Does it make sense? Is it defensible? Or is it unclear as to what the company does?

FORM 8-K

A public company is required to file a Form 8-K for any material event. This could be a merger or an announcement of failure to receive government approval on a drug.

A company has some discretion on what constitutes a material event. However, with the Congressional reforms of 2002, there are more items a company is required to disclose, such as the reasons for the resignation of the auditor and off-balance-sheet debts.

As for short sellers, they would be alerted to see the following:

- Resignation of the auditor: Did the auditor find problems with the company? Was the company pressuring the auditor?

- Resignation of senior executives: Is there turmoil at the top?
- Drop in a Company's Credit Rating: The company's financing is likely to become more expensive.
- Loss of a major customer: A customer that represents at least 10 percent of revenues.

PRESS RELEASES

The regulation of press releases is relatively lax. Short sellers, though, can gleam crucial information from them.

What short sellers are looking for is a company that engages in hype. Examples:

- Flamboyant language ("revolutionize," "unprecedented," "incredible," "never before")
- The Next . . . ("the next Microsoft," "the Next Amgen")
- Big claims ("market potential of $10 billion in the next three years")
- In an industry that is prone to scams (mining, medical drugs, technology)

An earnings release can provide tidbits of information for short sellers. The short seller likes to focus on the headline and the first couple of paragraphs. It is here where the company wants to emphasize its main points.

Short sellers are alerted when, in the earnings release, a company only discloses the income statement. The balance sheet might later be disclosed in the company's 10-Q or 10-K. Such disjointed disclosure makes it more difficult for short sellers (and any investor) to engage in effective analysis.

Pro forma earnings are yet another red flag. If a company is focusing on this—and not on the GAAP earnings—then short sellers might think the company is trying to brush over problems. For the most part, pro forma earnings are quite vague. It is easy for a company to make adjustments—and in some cases, turn a loss into a gain.

Most short sellers consider pro forma earnings to be useless. The SEC seems to agree. This is what it says about pro forma earnings on its Web site:

> "[T]hey may not convey a true and accurate picture of a company's financial well-being. They often highlight only positive information. And because 'pro forma' information doesn't have to follow established accounting rules, it can be very difficult to compare a company's 'pro forma' financial information to prior periods or to other companies."

FORM S-1: INITIAL PUBLIC OFFERINGS

An initial public offering (IPO) is the first time a company sells shares to the public. It is typically a big event with lots of hype. During boom times, an IPO can surge 100 percent or more on the first day of trading—as was common during the crazy days of the late 1990s.

Short sellers definitely find opportunity with overinflated IPOs. The big problem is timing. A stock can be at an excessively high price for a long time—and as a result, choke short sellers.

That is why smart short sellers will get a copy of the Form S-1, which is known as the prospectus. This is required for any IPO, but many investors just throw it away and bet their money on hope and greed.

Some of the key areas a short seller focuses on with the S-1 include:

Cover: The underwriter is the Wall Street firm that manages the IPO. In many cases, there will be a group of firms. Short sellers look for underwriters that are obscure or fairly small. The reason is that they typically do not have enough firepower to provide enough after-market trading to keep the stock increasing.

Interestingly enough, a company might not even have an underwriter. This is known as a direct IPO because the company is selling its shares directly to the public. Short sellers really like these types of offerings because there is very little if any after-market support.

The S-1 cover will show a price range for the IPO. It might be something like $12 to $14 per share. A short seller wants to see this range fall—or have the number of shares being offered be reduced. This is an indication of flagging demand.

Generally, an IPO is marketed to institutional and wealthy investors. The underwriter will make its pitch to these investors at road shows throughout the country. Over a few months, the underwriters will get indications of interest, and this is reflected in the price range. Thus, a fall in the range means that the road show is not going very well.

Risk Factors: A short seller will look for big lawsuits, intense competition, and any defaults on debt.

Use of Proceeds: This is often a vague statement such as "general purposes." But there might be a large amount to pay off debt. This means there is less money for the company to execute its business model.

Selling Shareholders: The executives, directors, and major shareholders must disclose any sale of stock in the IPO. A short seller will be alerted if, say, 30 percent or more of the IPO comes from selling shareholders. This is an indication that they are bailing out.

Lock-Up: An IPO will usually have this clause, which prevents all insiders from selling their shares for a period of time (the rule is six months). The rationale is that if these insiders started selling, it would be incredible pressure on the stock price.

Then again, this selling pressure is really delayed for six months. Many short sellers will wait a few weeks before this time period and take short positions in expectation of dumping of company shares.

Another form of an IPO is a spin-off. With this transaction, a company will sell a division of its business to the public and raise money in the process. This usually means an S-1 must be filed.

Studies indicate that a spin-off can be a good investment. Reasons include: analysts have an easier time understanding the overall business (that is, there are not as many moving parts); the company is not stifled by the bureaucracy; it is easier to incentivize management; and some capital is raised in the process.

However, there is a variation of the spin-off that is usually not a good investment: the tracking stock. Why? The big problem is that an investor in a tracking stock owns nothing; instead, the parent company retains ultimate control. Essentially, a tracking stock tracks the performance of the division of the parent company.

Other problems include:

- No takeover premium: Who would want to launch a takeover of a tracking stock, if purchase of the stock would not mean ownership in the division? There is no reason to do this, and it can put a damper on the valuation.

- Corporate governance: There are conflict problems. A tracking stock does not have its own board of directors. Rather, the parent's board is in control. So whose interests are being served? Chances are it is the parent's interests.

Finally, the issuance of a tracking stock is a common sign of a market top. So it was no surprise that there was a flurry of these offerings in the late 1990s.

CONCLUSION

There are hundreds of forms a company can file. But the ones we have looked at in the past few chapters are the key. In some cases, a company might have industry-specific forms that are worth considering (this is the case with banks and utilities, for example).

In the next chapter, we go away from fundamental analysis and take a look at technical analysis.

TECHNICAL ANALYSIS

Throughout much of this book, we have discussed fundamental analysis. This is when a short seller looks at a company's financial statements, product line, management team,
business model, and so on to glean information about how that
company operates and how well it's doing.

But there is another approach: technical analysis. On the face
of it, the process is very simple, that is, looking at the chart of a
company's price and volume history. Of course, short sellers
have developed many sophisticated techniques for technical
analysis, and they often require advanced software systems.

Keep in mind that of the two approaches, technical analysis
is often held with less esteem. Some investors think it is tanta-
mount to pure voodoo.

Despite all this, the fact remains that many investors and
short sellers follow technical analysis. Even the smart ones (and
they do not practice voodoo, either).

In this chapter, we look at the basic concepts of technical
analysis.

SOME HISTORY

Technical analysis has been in existence for several hundred
years. It can be quite tedious to use. However, this has become
less so with the emergence of the Internet, which has spawned a
variety of good charting Web sites.

Ultimately, technical analysis is about patterns. On the most basic level, if a company is experiencing problems, the stock price is likely to fall as investors move out of the stock. With technical analysis, the premise is that patterns continue for a while. It might not be for a long time—such as a year, but a pattern might last a few months, giving the investor time to make a profit.

The fact that technical analysis is geared for short-term moves is a big reason short sellers use this methodology. Generally, most short sellers look for quick profits, not long-term gains. A crucial reason is the costs of being short.

BASIC CHART TYPES

If something has a price and volume that changes over time, you can create a chart for it. It might be a stock index, like the S&P 500, or the price of gold.

All charts have the stock price on the upward sloping bar and the time on the bottom bar, as seen in Figure 11.1.

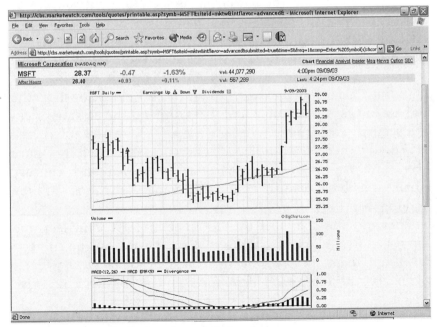

FIGURE 11.1.   A basic chart for technical analysis.

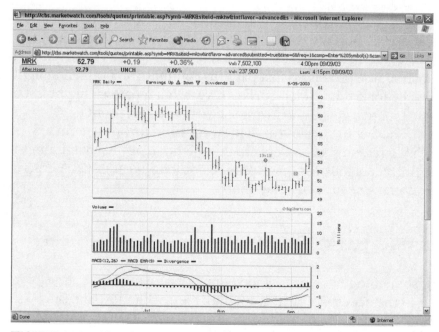

FIGURE 11.2.   This chart of Merck is an example of a bar chart.

One chart type is the bar chart, as seen in Figure 11.2. For each time period, there is a bar that shows the high and low price of the security. The bar that sticks out to the right is the price the security closed at. In some cases, there might be a line that sticks to the left, which is the stock's opening price.

A line chart, which is seen at Figure 11.3, does not show the high or low, but is a simple line that connects the closing prices of a security over time.

Finally, there are candlestick charts, as indicated in Figure 11.4. The origins of these charts are from sixteenth century Japan and have exotic sounding names, such as "Three Buddha Top," and the "Doji Star." These are effective tools— but beyond the scope of the book. If interested in learning about candlestick charts, there is a good book on the subject: *Japanese Candlestick Charting Techniques: A Contemporary Guide to the Ancient Investment Techniques of the Far East* by Steve Nison.

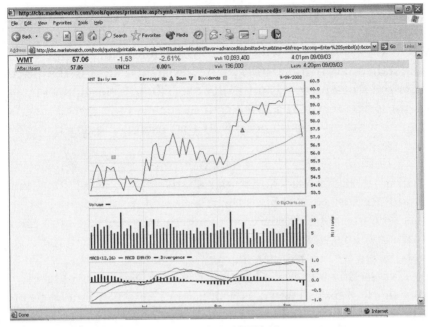

FIGURE 11.3. An·example of a line chart of Wal-Mart.

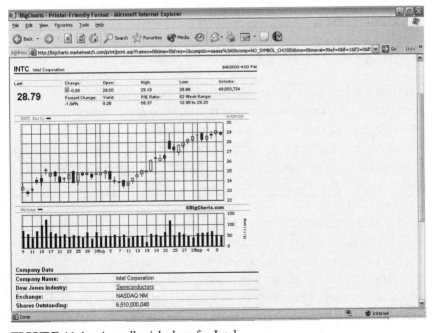

FIGURE 11.4. A candlestick chart for Intel.

SUPPORT AND RESISTANCE LEVELS

A technical analyst will try to determine the support and resistance levels for a stock. The resistance level is the price that the stock price has difficulty exceeding. The support level is the price at which a stock cannot seem to fall through. It is the support and resistance levels that establish a stock's trading range.

Look at Figure 11.5. The stock price of XYZ, on several occasions, has moved to $50 per share on three occasions, but could not surpass it. This is the resistance level. The stock price has fallen to $40 per share on two occasions, but has not fallen through. This would be the support level, and the trading range is between $40 to $50 per share.

Notice Figure 11.6. The stock price has gone past $40 to $35 per share. This is known as a break-out, and is a crucial thing that short sellers look at. There is no longer support at $40. Eventually, XYZ will create a new trading range. But with this break-out, it would certainly interest short sellers and could be an entry point to establish a short position in XYZ.

THE TREND IS YOUR FRIEND

There's an old saying on Wall Street that goes: "The trend is your friend." For short sellers, if they see a deteriorating trend line in a stock, this is a sign to short the stock.

How do you draw a trend line? Look at Figure 11.7. There are two trend lines: one for the resistance (the highs of the stock) and one for the support (the lows of the stock). Short sellers want to naturally see a declining trend line. In other words, the stock is hitting lower highs and lower lows.

Drawing trend lines is subjective. It can be different depending on the time period of the chart. For the most part, technical analysts will take a short view, say the last three or six months. You can also use the Web to help generate trend lines, such as *www.bigcharts.com*.

Stock Price

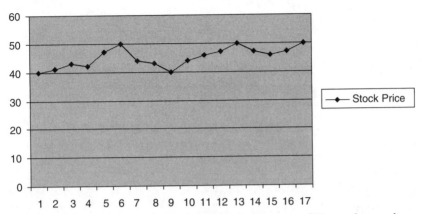

FIGURE 11.5. In this chart, the stock has a resistance at $50 per chart and a support level of $40 per share.

Stock Price

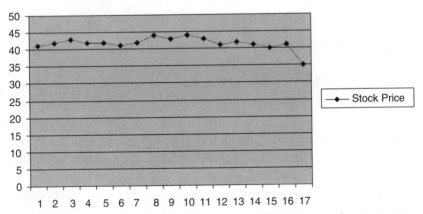

FIGURE 11.6. In this case, the stock has broken out of its trading range onto the downside.

MOVING AVERAGES

Moving averages tend to smooth out a series of prices to make it easier to identify patterns. A moving average is adjusted based on each time interval. For example, suppose you have a two-day moving average. In the past two days, the stock price was at $8

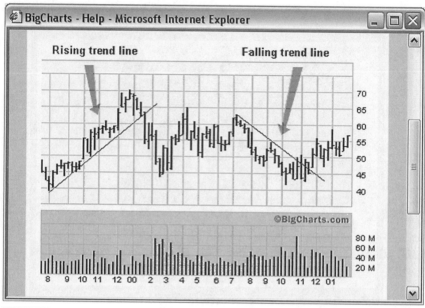

FIGURE 11.7.   Of course, technical analysts want to find falling trend lines.

and $9. The average would be $8.5. The next day, the stock price moves to $10. The two-day moving average would compute the two prior closes: $9 and $10, for an average of $9.5. For purposes of the chart, the last two data points would be $8.5 and $9.5.

A short seller will select a time frame for a moving average. Common ones include 21, 50, 150, and 200 days. Generally, the more volatile the stock, the longer the time frame employed.

A short seller might compare the current stock price to, say, the 150-day moving average. If the current stock price is below the moving average, this would be a negative sign and a possible short.

BEARISH CHART PATTERNS

There are myriad bearish chart patterns that short sellers track. If you want to explore such detail, look at the Resources sidebar, which highlights top books on technical analysis.

The following are some of the main bearish charts:

Double Top: This occurs when a stock hits two consecutive highs—at about the same price level—with a small trough in between (10 percent to 20 percent drop). The bearish case is reinforced if prior to the double top, there was a general uptrend in the stock for several months. Also, it is a bearish sign if the second top is on lighter volume.

Rising Wedge: The trading range is wide at the bottom and then, as prices increase, the trading range shrinks. This lasts anywhere from three to six months, and there is increasingly lower volume. A short seller looks for the support line to be broken on heavier volume.

Head and Shoulders Top: In this chart pattern, there are three peaks. The left and right peaks are at similar prices and the middle peak is at higher levels. The bearish trend is reinforced if the right peak is on a relatively lower volume.

VOLUME

Volume represents the numbers of shares bought and sold. Volume is a key factor for technical analysts. There's an old saying on Wall Street: Volume typically precedes changes in price.

Think of it as a tug-a-war between bears and bulls. Bulls are optimistic and buying stock. The bears are negative and selling out. Generally, if there is more buying volume, this should boost the stock price and vice versa.

A good volume indicator is the Accumulation/Distribution Line (ADL). The inventor is Marc Chaikin, who formulated a quite complex formula to measure the impact of volume. Thankfully, many online charting Web sites make the calculations for you.

To see if the ADL is bearish, there must be an uptrend in the stock. But, after this move, if the ADL begins to fall, it signals a potential fall in the stock price.

ARITHMETIC AND LOGARITHMIC SCALES

Logarithmic? You probably didn't want to rehash nightmares from math class. But it is important to know the difference between charts that are based on arithmetic and logarithmic scales.

By far, the most common chart is on the arithmetic scale. With this, a point move is the same distance regardless of the stock price. Example: Suppose Big Corp.'s stock price is $80 and it moves up $1. Small Corp., on the other hand, has a stock price of $2 and its stock price goes up by $1 on. On a chart, the $1 move is the same distance for both stocks.

The logarithmic method takes into account the percentage move. Thus, under this system, the move of Small Corp. will be much bigger than the one for Big Corp.

For volatile stocks, it is usually a good idea to use the logarithmic scale for charting.

ADVANCED TECHNICAL INDICATORS

Some of the other popular indicators for short sellers include:

Bollinger Bands: John Bollinger is a leading authority on technical analysis. One of his main contributions is based on his namesake, Bollinger Bands.

His premise is that stocks tend to trade in a range until there is some type of break-out. His chart has two bands—upper and lower—based on a statistical concept called standard deviation. He also has a 21-day moving average.

A short seller looks mainly at when a stock breaks below the lower band.

Stochastics: The mastermind behind this technique was George C. Lane, who made his findings in the 1950s. What stochastics measure is a stock's overall momentum. Is it in a bearish move or bullish move? This is measured numerically from 0 to 100. If a stochastic shoots above 80, it is a sign that the stock is overbought and poised for a fall, although you might want to wait until the stochastics comes back down to or past 80.

Moving Average Convergence-Divergence (MACD): This creates a centerline on a chart based on a formula—typically the 26-day and 12-day moving averages. The centerline occillates above and below zero.

RESOURCES FOR TECHNICAL ANALYSIS

Technical analysis is a well-developed field of investing. If interested in exploring further, here are some very helpful resources:

- *www.stockcharts.com*
- *www.bigcharts.com*
- Gary Smith's column on *thestreet.com*
- Robert Edwards's book *Technical Analysis of Stock Trends*
- John Murphy's book *The Visual Investor: How to Spot Market Trends*
- Thomas Bulkowski's book *Encyclopedia of Chart Patterns*
- *Technical Analysis of Stocks and Commodities* magazine

A short seller is encouraged if the centerline moves below zero—especially if the centerline had been above zero for several weeks.

CONCLUSION

Even if short sellers focus on fundamental factors, this does not mean they neglect technical analysis. Short sellers might use technical analysis to confirm their fundamental analysis. It might, for example, be a trigger for them to execute their orders—if they see a negative chart forming.

INDEX

About the Author

Tom Taulli is founder of the pioneering online investment company WebIPO. He is the author or coauthor of a number of investment books, including *The Streetsmart Guide to Short Selling*, *Tapping Into Wireless*, and others.